STUDENT WORKBOOK

PHONICS INTERVENTION

AN INCREMENTAL DEVELOPMENT

LORNA
SIMMONS

SAXON PUBLISHERS, INC.

Phonics Intervention: *An Incremental Development*

Student Workbook

Printed in the United States of America.

ISBN: 1-56577-231-8

Senior Editor: Julie Webster
Assistant Editors: Mary Burleson and Kimberley Oman
Prepress Manager: Travis Rose
Project Leader: Angela Johnson
Typesetters: Kimberley Oman and Jan Stratton
Proofreaders: Megan Berry and Carolyn Teague
Art Supervisor: Nancy Rimassa
Graphic Artist: Wendy Chitwood

Second printing: February 2000

Reaching us via the Internet

WWW: http://www.saxonpub.com

E-mail: info@saxonpub.com

Saxon Publishers, Inc.
2450 John Saxon Blvd.
Norman, OK 73071

TABLE OF CONTENTS

Lesson Worksheets

Lesson Worksheets (continued)

Phonics Rules

Name ______________________________

Teacher's Initials ______

Consonant Preassessment

Phonics Intervention

1.	2.	3.	4.	5.
______	______	______	______	______
6.	**7.**	**8.**	**9.**	**10.**
______	______	______	______	______
11.	**12.**	**13.**	**14.**	**15.**
______	______	______	______	______
16.	**17.**	**18.**	**19.**	
______	______	______	______	

Name ______________________________

Teacher's Initials ______

Worksheet 1
Phonics Intervention
Consonants

1. ______________
2. ______________
3. ______________
4. ______________
5. ______________
6. ______________
7. ______________
8. ______________
9. ______________
10. ______________
11. ______________
12. ______________
13. ______________
14. ______________
15. ______________
16. ______________
17. ______________
18. ______________
19. ______________

Name ______________________________

Teacher's Initials ______

Worksheet 2
Phonics Intervention
Aa

Coding and Reading

1. a c t
2. a l p
3. a p t
4. b a n
5. c a p
6. d a m p
7. f a c t
8. f a d
9. g a g
10. g a p
11. j a b
12. h a s
13. r a m
14. s a p
15. v a t

Spelling

16. ______________
17. ______________
18. ______________
19. ______________
20. ______________

Vocabulary

21. ______________
22. ______________
23. ______________
24. ______________

Alphabetizing

25. cap ban alp

____

____

____

Name ______________________________

Teacher's Initials ______

Worksheet 3
Phonics Intervention
Ii

Coding and Reading

1. b i d
2. s i t
3. d i l l
4. d i m
5. c a n
6. f i b
7. f i l m
8. a s k
9. h i n t
10. h i s s
11. I
12. h i s
13. h i
14. l a b
15. a

Spelling

16. ______________
17. ______________
18. ______________
19. ______________
20. ______________

Vocabulary

21. ______________
22. ______________
23. ______________
24. ______________

Alphabetizing

25. ink hit fan

____

____

____

Name ______________________________

Teacher's Initials _____

Coding and Reading

1. b o b
2. b o n d
3. f i g
4. i s
5. c o t
6. g a s
7. s o
8. p i
9. j o t
10. l o t
11. m a s s
12. n o d
13. o x
14. w o k
15. y i p

Spelling

16. ______________
17. ______________
18. ______________
19. ______________
20. ______________

Vocabulary

21. ______________
22. ______________
23. ______________
24. ______________

Alphabetizing

25. go hi ox

____

____

____

Name ______________________________

Teacher's Initials ______

Worksheet 5
Phonics Intervention
Uu

Coding and Reading

1. hut
2. cud
3. bog
4. dub
5. flu
6. mad
7. as
8. pox
9. hum
10. sum
11. hi
12. pun
13. raft
14. rut
15. wig

Spelling

16. ______________
17. ______________
18. ______________
19. ______________
20. ______________

Vocabulary

21. ______________
22. ______________
23. ______________
24. ______________

Alphabetizing

25. pun rut bud

____

____

____

Name ______________________________

Teacher's Initials ______

Worksheet 6
Phonics Intervention
Ee

Coding and Reading

1. b e
2. b e g
3. c a s t
4. f e l l
5. f o g
6. f u s s
7. t e x t
8. h e
9. i l l
10. k e p t
11. l e t
12. p a s s
13. p e g
14. r e v
15. s o p

Spelling

16. ______________
17. ______________
18. ______________
19. ______________
20. ______________

Vocabulary

21. ______________
22. ______________
23. ______________
24. ______________

Alphabetizing

25. he egg peg

____

____

____

Name ______________________________

Teacher's Initials ______

Worksheet 7
Phonics Intervention
Blends

Coding and Reading

1. b a s k
2. s c r a m
3. b l o t
4. c l a s p
5. c r e s t
6. d r i l l
7. f l i t
8. h a s
9. p l a n t
10. p r o
11. s p r i n t
12. s t u n t
13. t r o t
14. t r u m p
15. t w i g

Spelling

16. ______________
17. ______________
18. ______________
19. ______________
20. ______________

Vocabulary

21. ______________
22. ______________
23. ______________
24. ______________

Alphabetizing

25. cat fax

bat______________

____

dab______________

____

gal______________

Name ______________________________

Teacher's Initials ______

Coding and Reading

1. by
2. cliff
3. cuff
4. dry
5. flop
6. he
7. ply
8. pry
9. spry
10. lynx
11. tad
12. tiff
13. trod
14. tuft
15. we

Spelling

16. ______
17. ______
18. ______
19. ______
20. ______

Vocabulary

21. ______
22. ______
23. ______
24. ______

Alphabetizing

25. tug can peg

______

fun ______

______

sit ______

______

Name ______________________________

Teacher's Initials ______

Worksheet 9
Phonics Intervention

th, ~~th~~, thr

Coding and Reading

1. fifth
2. filth
3. fly
4. froth
5. moth
6. bath
7. myth
8. path
9. than
10. them
11. thin
12. thrift
13. throb
14. thud
15. thug

Spelling

16. ______________
17. ______________
18. ______________
19. ______________
20. ______________

Vocabulary

21. ______________
22. ______________
23. ______________
24. ______________

Alphabetizing

25. log ham cap

am ______________

____

____

jet ______________

____

Name ______________________________

Teacher's Initials ______

Worksheet 10
Phonics Intervention
sh, shr

Coding and Reading

1. a s h
2. b r u s h
3. h u s h
4. c r u s h
5. d a s h
6. f l e s h
7. f l u s h
8. m e s h
9. p l u s h
10. s h e
11. s h o d
12. s h r e d
13. s h r i l l
14. s h y
15. t h e f t

Spelling

16. ____________
17. ____________
18. ____________
19. ____________
20. ____________

Vocabulary

21. ____________
22. ____________
23. ____________
24. ____________

Alphabetizing

25. at fin dog

____

bet ____________

____

____

lot ____________

Name ______________________________

Teacher's Initials ______

Worksheet 11
Phonics Intervention
ch, ch, ch

Coding and Reading

1. chap
2. chat
3. chef
4. chip
5. chomp
6. chop
7. flinch
8. inch
9. lunch
10. crypt
11. much
12. ranch
13. splash
14. so
15. that

Spelling

16. ______________
17. ______________
18. ______________
19. ______________
20. ______________

Vocabulary

21. ______________
22. ______________
23. ______________
24. ______________

Alphabetizing

25. cut ban so

____

____

fit ______________

hat ______________

____

Name ________________________________

Teacher's Initials ______

Worksheet 12

Phonics Intervention

Spelling Initial and Medial /k/

Spelling with *c* and *k*

When spelling the initial and medial /k/ sound:
k is usually found before *e*, *i*, and *y*;
c is usually found before *a*, *o*, *u*, or any consonant.

Spelling, Coding, and Reading

1. _amp
2. _ash
3. _loth
4. _on
5. _runch
6. _elp
7. _id
8. _iss
9. du_t
10. s_an
11. s_rap
12. s_ript
13. s_imp
14. s_it
15. s_y

Spelling

16. ____________________

17. ____________________

18. ____________________

19. ____________________

20. ____________________

Vocabulary

21. ____________________

22. ____________________

23. ____________________

24. ____________________

Alphabetizing

25. got egg kit

dig____________________

____

____

____

me____________________

Name ______________________________

Teacher's Initials ______

Worksheet 13
Phonics Intervention
¢k

Coding and Reading

1. shack
2. neck
3. mock
4. flock
5. buck
6. tack
7. me
8. check
9. wick
10. stock

Spelling

11. ______________
12. ______________
13. ______________
14. ______________
15. ______________

Vocabulary

16. ______________
17. ______________
18. ______________
19. ______________

Alphabetizing

20. sick • tab (page 72)
tablet • tactic (page 73)
tactile • take (page 74)

tack ____________

Reading Comprehension

(Worksheet 13, continued)

It is a fact that the filth in the pig's pen smells bad.

21. The filth in the pig's pen ____.

22. Is it a fact that the pig's pen smells? ________________________________

____

____

Name ______________________________

Teacher's Initials ______

Worksheet 14
Phonics Intervention
Sight Words, 1

New Sight Words

1. want
2. of
3. where
4. are
5. was
6. from
7. to
8. what
9. said
10. were

Spelling

11. ______________
12. ______________
13. ______________
14. ______________
15. ______________

Vocabulary

16. ______________
17. ______________
18. ______________
19. ______________

Reading Comprehension

The stock will get grass at the back by the gulch.

20. What will the stock get? ______________________________

____

____

21. Where is the grass? ______________________________

____

____

Name ______________________________

Teacher's Initials ______

Worksheet 15
Phonics Intervention
vc′|cv and vc|cv′

Coding and Reading

1. insect
2. classic
3. stick
4. picnic
5. cosmic
6. indent
7. unless
8. until
9. upset
10. admit

Spelling

11. ____________
12. ____________
13. ____________
14. ____________
15. ____________

Vocabulary

16. ____________
17. ____________
18. ____________
19. ____________

Alphabetizing

20. foster • fox-trot (page 41)
frail • fray (page 42)
free • freeze (page 43)

fox ____________

Reading Comprehension

(Worksheet 15, continued)

Beth will admit that she was by the thick, damp grass in the fog.

21. Where was Beth? ______________________________

____

____

22. What was damp? ______________________________

____

____

Name ______________________________

Teacher's Initials ______

Worksheet 16
Phonics Intervention

ng

Coding and Reading

1. fang

2. length

3. chin

4. sting

5. clung

6. pack

7. candid

8. pro

9. thing

10. shrink

Spelling

11. ______________

12. ______________

13. ______________

14. ______________

15. ______________

Vocabulary

16. ______________

17. ______________

18. ______________

19. ______________

Alphabetizing

20. flap • flax (page 36)
fleck • flint (page 37)
flip • flu (page 38)

fling ______________

Reading Comprehension

The fox pups hid in the grass as Jan got a candid shot of the fox with his fang hung in the stick.

21. What was hung in the stick? ______________________

____

____

22. Where were the fox pups? ______________________

____

____

Name ____________________

Teacher's Initials ______

Worksheet 17
Phonics Intervention
v̄–¢

Coding and Reading

1. f a m e
2. p r i d e
3. t r o m b o n e
4. t h e m e
5. m u t e
6. s h a m e
7. c h i m e
8. n o
9. s l i n g
10. l a c k

Spelling

11. ____________
12. ____________
13. ____________
14. ____________
15. ____________

Vocabulary

16. ____________
17. ____________
18. ____________
19. ____________

Alphabetizing

20. bag • bake (page 12)
baking • ball (page 13)
ballad • band (page 14)

bait ____________

Reading Comprehension

(Worksheet 17, continued)

Steve left his theme in the back of his dad's truck. It was a bad excuse, and his theme was late, so Miss Blake gave him a bad grade.

21. Where was Steve's theme? ______________________________

____

____

22. What was late? ______________________________

____

____

Name ______________________________

Teacher's Initials ______

Worksheet 18

Phonics Intervention

Vowel Digraphs (āi̸, āy̸, ēa̸, ēe̸, ēi̸, ēy̸, īe̸, ōa̸, ōe̸, ūe̸)

Coding and Reading

1. b a i t
2. s w a y
3. b l e a c h
4. f l e e
5. s e i z e
6. c h i m n e y
7. b r i n g
8. t h r o a t
9. s a v e
10. r a c k

Spelling

11. ______________
12. ______________
13. ______________
14. ______________
15. ______________

Vocabulary

16. ______________
17. ______________
18. ______________
19. ______________

Alphabetizing

20. valve • vapor (page 119)
    valid • value (page 118)
    utter • vale (page 117)

    vain ______________

Reading Comprehension

(Worksheet 18, continued)

Kim will use bleach to clean the sink. She will not breathe the air near the bleach as it will make Kim's throat feel bad. The fumes are strong!

21. What will Kim use to clean the sink? ______________________________

____

____

22. What will feel bad if Kim breathes the air near the bleach? ______________

____

____

Name ______________________________

Teacher's Initials ______

Worksheet 19
Phonics Intervention
Spelling with ā–¢ and ay
Spelling with ū–¢ and ue

Spelling

ā–¢

1. ______________

2. ______________

3. ______________

____

____

‖ay

4. ______________

5. ______________

6. ______________

____

____

ū–¢

7. ______________

8. ______________

9. ______________

____

____

‖ue

10. ______________

11. ______________

12. ______________

____

____

Vocabulary

13. ______________

14. ______________

15. ______________

16. ______________

Alphabetizing

17. shave same state

____

____

____

Name ______________________________

Teacher's Initials ______

Worksheet 20
Phonics Intervention
Spelling with ee

Spelling

ee

1. ______________
2. ______________
3. ______________
4. ______________
5. ______________
6. ______________

____

____

||ee

7. ______________
8. ______________
9. ______________
10. ______________
11. ______________
12. ______________

____

____

Vocabulary

13. ______________
14. ______________
15. ______________
16. ______________

Alphabetizing

17. steer sneer seed

____

____

____

Name ______________________________

Teacher's Initials ______

Worksheet 21
Phonics Intervention
Sight Words, 2

Sight Word Review

1. ______________
2. ______________
3. ______________
4. ______________
5. ______________
6. ______________
7. ______________
8. ______________
9. ______________
10. ______________

New Sight Words

11. does
12. some
13. who
14. come
15. do
16. put
17. one
18. don't
19. says
20. didn't

Reading Comprehension

Mom said Sal must come home from the beach by one, but Sal didn't make it in time. Sal said she was not late, but it was a fib. Mom does not like it if Sal fibs, so she had to do some chores and then go to bed. If Sal fibs next time, she will not get to go back to the beach.

21. What time must Sal be home from the beach? ____________________

____

____

22. Who gets mad if Sal fibs? ____________________________

____

____

Name ______________________________

Teacher's Initials ______

Coding and Reading

1. verb
2. blunder
3. hermit
4. slumber
5. tweet
6. seam
7. dinner
8. gait
9. medley
10. oar

Spelling

11. ____________
12. ____________
13. ____________
14. ____________
15. ____________

Vocabulary

16. ____________
17. ____________
18. ____________
19. ____________

Alphabetizing

20. blunder belt boat

____

____

____

Reading Comprehension

(Worksheet 22, continued)

Joe's hammer bent the nail and made a crack in the shelf his sister gave him. He had to pry the nail from the shelf and put some glue in the crack. After a bit, the glue held, and Joe felt better. He did not want his sister to see the crack in the shelf.

21. What made the shelf crack? ______________________________

____

____

22. Who gave Joe the shelf? ______________________________

____

____

Name ______________________________

Teacher's Initials ______

Worksheet 23
Phonics Intervention

ir

Coding and Reading

1. shirk
2. first
3. swirl
4. free
5. chirp
6. distinct
7. expert
8. rubbish
9. ferret
10. wire

Spelling

11. ______________
12. ______________
13. ______________
14. ______________
15. ______________

Vocabulary

16. ______________
17. ______________
18. ______________
19. ______________

Alphabetizing

20. end expert egg

____

____

____

Reading Comprehension

A bluebird sits in a birch tree. Her meal is in the dirt. The bluebird hopes to seize an insect from the dirt and get her meal. She will lay eggs in a nest of grass and stems after she eats some fruit from a peach tree.

21. What does a bluebird eat? ______________________________

____

____

22. Where will the bluebird lay her eggs? ______________________________

____

____

Name ______________________________

Teacher's Initials ______

Worksheet 24
Phonics Intervention

ur

Coding and Reading

1. b u r s t

2. s p u r

3. t u r k e y

4. m u r m u r

5. p l e a t

6. d i s t u r b

7. d i r t

8. f u r n i s h

9. p u r e

10. h e r r i n g

Spelling

11. ______________

12. ______________

13. ______________

14. ______________

15. ______________

Vocabulary

16. ______________

17. ______________

18. ______________

19. ______________

Alphabetizing

20. curb cot cat

____

____

____

Reading Comprehension

(Worksheet 24, continued)

Curt was home with his big sister, Fern. Fern put burgers on the grill. Curt went to the grill to help her. Fern went inside to get some pepper, and the grill burst into flames. Curt ran to get Fern to soak the fire with a hose. The burgers were black and wet, so Curt and Fern had turkey T.V. dinners. Fern will not stray from the flame next time.

21. Who put the burgers on the grill? ______________________

____

____

22. What did Fern go inside to get? ______________________

____

____

Name ______________________________

Teacher's Initials ______

Worksheet 25
Phonics Intervention

qu

Coding and Reading

1. q u a c k

2. q u e s t

3. s q u i r m

4. s q u i s h

5. s q u a r e

6. s q u e a k

7. q u a i n t

8. q u o t e

9. n u t m e g

10. i n v e s t

Spelling

11. ______________

12. ______________

13. ______________

14. ______________

15. ______________

Vocabulary

16. ______________

17. ______________

18. ______________

19. ______________

Alphabetizing

20. turn fern gill

burn______________

____

____

herd______________

____

Reading Comprehension

(Worksheet 25, continued)

A fat rat was in the trap. The rat was quick and ran up to eat some of the cream pie that sat on Dad's plate. Dad ran after the rat but was not as fast. He put some cheese in a trap and set this trap next to the pie. The fat rat ran back to seize some more cream pie, but the trap got him. Dad was glad to trap the rat, but he didn't get cream pie at dinner.

21. Where was the cream pie? ______________________________

____

____

22. Who got to eat some cream pie? ______________________________

____

____

Name ______________________________

Teacher's Initials ______

Worksheet 26
Phonics Intervention

wh

Coding and Reading

1. w h i f f

2. w h i r l

3. w h e l p

4. w h e e l

5. w h e a t

6. w h i s k e r

7. w h y

8. s q u e a l

9. w h e e z e

10. w h i m p e r

Spelling

11. ______________

12. ______________

13. ______________

14. ______________

15. ______________

Vocabulary

16. ______________

17. ______________

18. ______________

19. ______________

Alphabetizing

20. from was where

are ______________

____

said ______________

____

____

Reading Comprehension

(Worksheet 26, continued)

One day I rode my bike to the beach with my dog, Whiskers. I like to go to the beach to see the big white whales. As we got close to shore, we got a whiff of the sweet sea air. The wheels of my bike got stuck in the sand, and I had to leave it. I didn't want to leave, but Whiskers does not like the big white whales as much as I do.

21. Where did I ride my bike? ______________________________

____

____

22. What did Whiskers want to do? ______________________________

____

____

Name ______________________________

Teacher's Initials _____

Worksheet 27
Phonics Intervention
-s

Coding and Reading

1. stumps
2. chains
3. weeds
4. shirts
5. while
6. goats
7. toads
8. quite
9. napkins
10. curls

Spelling

11. ____________
12. ____________
13. ____________
14. ____________
15. ____________

Vocabulary

16. ____________
17. ____________
18. ____________
19. ____________

Alphabetizing

20. says want what

of ____________

____

____

were ____________

____

Sentence Completion *(Worksheet 27, continued)*

stumps chains weeds shirts while goats toads quite napkins curls

21. The ____________ in the back need to be cut.

22. Put her red ____________ in the pink-and-white bag with her blue pants.

23. The ____________ eat grass, hay, and weeds.

24. Put the ____________ on his tires so he will not slide.

25. The man cut five trees but left the ____________.

Name ______________________________

Teacher's Initials ______

Worksheet 28
Phonics Intervention
-ing, -less

Coding and Reading

1. sifting
2. meatless
3. raining
4. singing
5. teaching
6. squinting
7. backless
8. thundering
9. burning
10. wheels

Spelling

11. ______________
12. ______________
13. ______________
14. ______________
15. ______________

Vocabulary

16. ______________
17. ______________
18. ______________
19. ______________

Alphabetizing

20. tray see lung

chip

____

mask

____

____

Sentence Completion

sifting meatless raining singing teaching
squinting backless thundering burning wheels

21. The dogs hid under the bed while Max was ______________ with Seth.

22. Mister Black is ______________ Zack to sing.

23. Deb's white prom dress is ______________.

24. The burgers were ______________ on the grill.

25. The ______________ on Jake's truck were bent.

Name ____________________

Teacher's Initials ______

Worksheet 29
Phonics Intervention
-ed

Coding and Reading

1. filmed
2. melted
3. quills
4. seeded
5. shrinking
6. soaked
7. strayed
8. hatless
9. turned
10. whirled

Spelling

11. ____________
12. ____________
13. ____________
14. ____________
15. ____________

Vocabulary

16. ____________
17. ____________
18. ____________
19. ____________

Alphabetizing

20. stop sped snail

slap ____________

____

____

square ____________

____

Sentence Completion

filmed melted quills seeded shrinking
soaked strayed hatless turned whirled

21. Dad ____________ Frank as he left home to go to the prom.

22. The butter ____________ in the sun.

23. The girl was ____________ after running in the rain to get her mail.

24. The pup strayed off the trail and came back with ____________ in his nose.

25. Joel ____________ the meat while Fran toasted the hot dog buns.

Name ____________________

Teacher's Initials ______

Worksheet 30
Phonics Intervention
Dictionary Coding

Coding and Reading

1. k n o w ____________
2. p a c t ____________
3. w r i t e ____________
4. g n e i s s ____________
5. c r o q u e t ____________
6. / ĭ z /
7. / ŭ v /
8. / e r t h /
9. / f l ō t /
10. / p ō´ n ē t ā l /

Spelling

11. ____________
12. ____________
13. ____________
14. ____________
15. ____________

Vocabulary

16. ____________
17. ____________
18. ____________
19. ____________

Alphabetizing

20. board bunch black

bit ____________

____

____

braid ____________

____

Sentence Completion

know pact write gneiss croquet

21. I ____________ the way to the store.

22. Let's play a game of ______________.

23. Who will ____________ the name on the sheet?

24. The girls made a ___________ with each **other** (ŭth′ er).

25. ______________ is a type of rock.

Name ________________________________

Teacher's Initials _____

Worksheet 31
Phonics Intervention
Sight Words, 3

Sight Word Review

1. ______________
2. ______________
3. ______________
4. ______________
5. ______________
6. ______________
7. ______________
8. ______________
9. ______________
10. ______________

New Sight Words

11. because
12. their
13. would
14. been
15. four
16. other
17. they
18. should
19. there
20. could

Sentence Completion

some who don't one put come didn't do does says

21. ___________ is playing the drums?

22. Where _________ I go to get some glue?

23. Three plus __________ is four.

24. ____________ make me **laugh** (lăf)!

25. __________ the trash in the black trash bag.

Name ____________________

Teacher's Initials ______

Worksheet 32
Phonics Intervention
ar = /ar/

Coding and Reading

1. arc
2. barber
3. scarlet
4. varmint
5. marsh
6. harvest
7. garment
8. barked
9. marketing
10. harmless

Spelling

11. ____________
12. ____________
13. ____________
14. ____________
15. ____________

Vocabulary

16. ____________
17. ____________
18. ____________
19. ____________

Alphabetizing

20. would their other could been

____

____

____

____

____

Reading Comprehension

A varmint was stealing from the barn and messing things up. The wheat seed was scattered on the top shelf where we keep it. The hay was on the dirt. Part of my dad's tar had spilled on the hay. My mom's scarf was missing. The varmint would sneak into the barn after dark. One time I went in, and it snarled at me. My dad set a wire box trap, and the next day the varmint was in it. The varmint was a skunk! Its fur was black with a white stripe. I am so glad I did not get sprayed!

21. What was scattered on the shelf? ______________________________

____

____

22. What **color** (kŭl′ er) is a skunk's fur? ______________________________

____

____

Name ______________________________

Teacher's Initials _____

Worksheet 33
Phonics Intervention
or = /or/

Coding and Reading

1. cork
2. chord
3. border
4. inform
5. torment
6. scorch
7. hornet
8. farming
9. thornless
10. sorted

Spelling

11. ______________
12. ______________
13. ______________
14. ______________
15. ______________

Vocabulary

16. ______________
17. ______________
18. ______________
19. ______________

Alphabetizing

20. to they goes put didn't

____

____

____

____

____

Reading Comprehension

(Worksheet 33, continued)

A stork is a bird that has long legs and a long beak. Some storks nest in trees. Storks eat insects, frogs, and snakes. Some **people** (pē′ pŭl) think that storks can bring luck, like a birth; others think that storks can bring bad luck after they leave. **Most** (mōst) people think these are just myths **though** (tħō).

21. What is a stork? ____________________

____

____

22. What do storks eat? ____________________

____

____

Name ______________________________

Teacher's Initials _____

Worksheet 34
Phonics Intervention
or = /er/

Coding and Reading

1. splendor
2. error
3. working
4. jar
5. tractor
6. or
7. vendor
8. parch
9. forth
10. worst

Spelling

11. ______________
12. ______________
13. ______________
14. ______________
15. ______________

Vocabulary

16. ______________
17. ______________
18. ______________
19. ______________

Alphabetizing

20. pact basked sifting whim quest

____

____

____

____

____

Reading Comprehension

One could **imagine** (ĭm ăj′ ŭn) my horror when I bumped into a robber in my home. He was just as shocked as I was. I screamed, and he ran. He did not look where he was going, so he ran into my plate glass **window** (wĭn′ dō) and fell on the carpet. The **police** (pŭ lēs′) came and got him.

21. Who did I run into? ______________________________

____

____

22. What did the robber run into? ______________________________

____

____

Name ______________________________

Teacher's Initials ______

Worksheet 35
Phonics Intervention
ar = /er/

Coding and Reading

1. c o l l a r
2. b u z z a r d
3. h a r b o r
4. g r a m m a r
5. a r m o r
6. c o l l a r d s
7. t a r
8. w o r l d
9. w a r m
10. w a r

Spelling

11. ____________________
12. ____________________
13. ____________________
14. ____________________
15. ____________________

Vocabulary

16. ____________________
17. ____________________
18. ____________________
19. ____________________

Alphabetizing

20. stumps murmur shirk verb sneer

____

____

____

____

____

Reading Comprehension

Mom made a list of the jobs she needs to do today:

- Go to the store and get mustard, peach nectar, starch for shirt collars, custard, and plastic hangers.
- Pick up a lock to keep **burglars** (ber′ glerz) from getting in.
- Make Josh do his grammar homework.
- Get ten dollars to pay June for the yard work.
- Get worms for Dad and Josh's fishing trip.
- Pick up a warm shirt for Josh.
- Fill up the car and tractor with gas.

21. Why does Mom need worms? ______________________________

____

____

22. What needs gas? ______________________________

____

____

Name ______________________________

Teacher's Initials ______

Coding and Reading

1. garland

2. fossil

3. distant

4. oppose

5. normal

6. collapse

7. skillet

8. confuse

9. velvet

10. confide

Spelling

11. ______________

12. ______________

13. ______________

14. ______________

15. ______________

Vocabulary

16. ______________

17. ______________

18. ______________

19. ______________

Alphabetizing

20. seize pride pang indent wick

____

____

____

____

____

Sentence Completion

(Worksheet 36, continued)

garland fossil distant oppose normal
collapse skillet confuse velvet confide

21. The rock had a ____________ of a leaf.

22. "Don't let the tent ______________ on the dog," said Carlos.

23. Linda's dad was frying ham in the ____________.

24. The dress was made of blue ____________.

25. Do not use big words and try to ______________ my son!

Name ______________________________

Teacher's Initials _____

Sight Word Review

1. ________________
2. ________________
3. ________________
4. ________________
5. ________________
6. ________________
7. ________________
8. ________________
9. ________________
10. ________________

New Sight Words

11. trouble
12. many
13. father
14. ocean
15. any
16. sure
17. brother
18. learn
19. buy
20. mother

Reading Comprehension

(Worksheet 37, continued)

My mother, brother, father, and I went to the ocean last week. We sifted **through** (thrū) the sand but didn't see many shells, so my mother let us buy some. There were many shells in the stores that I could not seem to **find** (fīnd) on the beach. It is less trouble buying shells, but it is more fun finding them. I am sure we will go back to the beach, and I hope to learn more each time we go.

21. Where did we go? ______________________________

____

____

22. Why did we buy shells? ______________________________

____

____

Name ______________________________

Teacher's Initials _____

Worksheet 38
Phonics Intervention
Spelling Final /k/

Spelling with *ck* and *k*

When spelling the final /k/ sound:
ck is found after a short vowel;
k is found after a consonant or a vowel digraph.

Spelling, Coding, and Reading

1. s l a ___
2. w e e ___
3. s i l ___
4. s p a r ___
5. c l i ___
6. s m o ___
7. h u n ___
8. p l u ___
9. s n a ___
10. w h i s ___
11. n i ___
12. p o r ___
13. t r a ___
14. d u s ___
15. m i l ___

Spelling

16. ____________________

17. ____________________

18. ____________________

19. ____________________

20. ____________________

Vocabulary

21. ____________________

22. ____________________

23. ____________________

24. ____________________

Alphabetizing

25. dim
    - ○ don't • eaves
    - ○ cub • dale
    - ○ desk • dock

Name ______________________________

Teacher's Initials ______

Worksheet 39
Phonics Intervention

<u>**oo**</u>

Coding and Reading

1. stood
2. drooping
3. broom
4. proof
5. scooped
6. swoop
7. hoofless
8. custom
9. hamper
10. garnish

Spelling

11. ______________
12. ______________
13. ______________
14. ______________
15. ______________

Vocabulary

16. ______________
17. ______________
18. ______________
19. ______________

Alphabetizing

20. moth

○ miss • munch
○ mass • mess
○ must • myth

Reading Comprehension

(Worksheet 39, continued)

Ned has been working hard, and he will soon **have** (hăv) a six-foot by four-foot room added to his home. In this room he will keep his stools, rags, paint, ladders, and some other tools that he will store on hooks. When Ned is working on the room, he forgets to eat lunch at noon. Ned likes to shoot hoops at dusk each day after he is **through** (thrū) working on his room.

21. What size will Ned's room be? ______________________________

____

____

22. Where will Ned keep his tools? ______________________________

____

____

Name ______________________________

Teacher's Initials ______

Worksheet 40
Phonics Intervention
"Wild Colt" Words

Coding and Reading

1. blind
2. both
3. child
4. colt
5. host
6. grind
7. mold
8. rind
9. scroll
10. too

Spelling

11. ________________
12. ________________
13. ________________
14. ________________
15. ________________

Vocabulary

16. ________________
17. ________________
18. ________________
19. ________________

Alphabetizing

20. flu
   ○ fill • hint
   ○ frost • jump
   ○ cash • fed

Reading Comprehension

(Worksheet 40, continued)

Kate needed to find her wild colt, who had torn his gate off its hooks. She drove by the old gold mine, the old fort, and the tool shed but could not find her wild colt anywhere. Kate drove for four more miles and then started home. When she got there, the wild colt was where he should be—in his pen eating his oats.

21. Where did Kate look after the gold mine? ______________________________

____

____

22. What was the wild colt eating when Kate came home? ____________________

____

____

Name ______________________________

Teacher's Initials ______

Worksheet 41
Phonics Intervention
Review of Combinations

Review

1. ______________
2. ______________
3. ______________
4. ______________
5. ______________
6. ______________
7. ______________
8. ______________
9. ______________
10. ______________

Spelling

11. ______________
12. ______________
13. ______________
14. ______________
15. ______________

Vocabulary

16. ______________
17. ______________
18. ______________
19. ______________

Alphabetizing

20. duct
   - ○ kid • list
   - ○ camp • day
   - ○ dent • fish

Name ______________________________

Teacher's Initials ______

Worksheet 42
Phonics Intervention
-er, -est

Coding and Reading

1. sweeter
2. shortest
3. fished
4. colder
5. finding
6. thickest
7. proofer
8. quickest
9. smartest
10. mildest

Spelling

11. ______________
12. ______________
13. ______________
14. ______________
15. ______________

Vocabulary

16. ______________
17. ______________
18. ______________
19. ______________

Alphabetizing

20. colt
   - ○ child • cost
   - ○ ban • cat
   - ○ cut • for

Sentence Completion

sweeter shortest fished colder finding
thickest proofer quickest smartest mildest

21. Steve's cake was _______________ than **sugar** (shoog′ er).

22. The _______________ book on the shelf is the one that Jayden will read next.

23. Justin _____________ in the pond and **caught** (kŏt) three fish.

24. Mike was _____________ than Lee, so Lee let him use her coat.

25. The ________________ person will choose players for the soccer team, and the **tallest** (tŏl′ əst) person will choose players for the tennis team.

Name ______________________________

Teacher's Initials ______

Worksheet 43
Phonics Intervention
Sight Words, 5

Sight Word Review

1. ____________
2. ____________
3. ____________
4. ____________
5. ____________
6. ____________
7. ____________
8. ____________
9. ____________
10. ____________

New Sight Words

11. give (live)
12. again (against)
13. young
14. only
15. door
16. walk
17. friend
18. enough
19. talk
20. have

Reading Comprehension

(Worksheet 43, continued)

My younger brother, who is four years old, has a true friend. This friend, who is older than we are, helped him learn to walk and talk. When my brother gets older, this friend will teach him to read too. This friend gives enough time to my brother so that he is the only friend my brother needs. When he walks in the door after work, my brother hugs him again and again. I hug my father too.

21. What did my brother's friend help him learn to do?

____

____

22. Who is my brother's friend? ______________________________

____

____

Name ______________________________

Teacher's Initials ______

Worksheet 44
Phonics Intervention
Floss Rule

Coding and Reading

1. t o ___

2. s c u ___

3. c r o ___

4. s t a ___

5. p r e ___

6. s h a ___

7. w e ___

8. w i ___

9. m o ___

10. s t u ___

Spelling

11. ________________

12. ________________

13. ________________

14. ________________

15. ________________

Vocabulary

16. ________________

17. ________________

18. ________________

19. ________________

Alphabetizing

20. again ________________ door

Reading Comprehension

(Worksheet 44, continued)

Bess has a math class that starts at nine. She does not feel well but does not want to miss her class. Bess needs to turn in an old test that she took last week. She sniffs and snorts and hopes that she is not ill for long. Bess may hand her test in and then go back home where she can rest.

21. What time does Bess's math class start?

____

____

22. What does she need to turn in? ______________________________

____

____

Name ____

Teacher's Initials _____

Worksheet 45
Phonics Intervention
´[bl¢

Coding and Reading

1. b a b b l e

2. f a b l e

3. g a m b l e

4. h o b b l e

5. m u m b l e

6. r u b l e

7. n i m b l e

8. s t a b l e

9. t r o o p

10. z o n e

Spelling

11. ____________________

12. ____________________

13. ____________________

14. ____________________

15. ____________________

Vocabulary

16. ____________________

17. ____________________

18. ____________________

19. ____________________

Alphabetizing

20. enough ____________________ friend

Reading Comprehension

(Worksheet 45, continued)

Kyle sat at the table and picked at his food. He did not like to grumble, but he didn't like scrambled eggs. If his mother had made poached eggs, he would have gobbled them up. Kyle mumbled when his mother asked if he would like more eggs. He wanted to make at least a feeble effort to act as if he liked the eggs because he did not want to hurt his mother's feelings.

21. What kind of eggs did Kyle like?

____

____

22. Did Kyle want more eggs? Why or why not? ____________________

____

____

Name ______________________________

Teacher's Initials ______

Worksheet 46
Phonics Intervention
´[dl¢, ´[pl¢

Coding and Reading

1. bridle
2. huddle
3. crumple
4. ladle
5. needle
6. ripple
7. sample
8. spindle
9. creak
10. squeeze

Spelling

11. ______________
12. ______________
13. ______________
14. ______________
15. ______________

Vocabulary

16. ______________
17. ______________
18. ______________
19. ______________

Alphabetizing

20. give ______________ have

Reading Comprehension

(Worksheet 46, continued)

Chris needed to buy Ann a gift. She wanted Ann to like the gift, so she asked her to make a list of things she would like. This is what Ann put on her list: bubble bath, a big red apple, needlework, a paddle for her boat, a book of riddles, a bag of marbles, a thimble, and a green candle. Chris was glad to have so much to choose from.

21. What kind of paddle did Ann want? ______________________________

____

____

22. Would Ann like a purple candle? ______________________________

____

____

Name ______________________________

Teacher's Initials ______

Worksheet 47
Phonics Intervention
´[flȼ, ´[glȼ, ´[plȼ, ´[tlȼ,
´[clȼ, ´[klȼ, ´[zlȼ

Coding and Reading

1. u n c l e

2. r i f l e

3. s t r u g g l e

4. f r e c k l e

5. t u s s l e

6. b e e t l e

7. m u z z l e

8. t r i f l e

9. g a r g l e

10. t h r o t t l e

Spelling

11. ______________

12. ______________

13. ______________

14. ______________

15. ______________

Vocabulary

16. ______________

17. ______________

18. ______________

19. ______________

Alphabetizing

20. only ______________ talk

Reading Comprehension

(Worksheet 47, continued)

A man wanted to rob a bank, but he stumbled on the steps as he entered the door. When he stumbled, he took a tumble and startled Jan, the teller. Jan screamed and hit the button that set off a horn. As the horn blasted, Steve and Karl tried to muffle it. Meanwhile, Lynn tried to help the man who stumbled. The man struggled with Lynn, but she held him on the rug. Jan yelled for Steve and Karl to help Lynn with the man. The three people held him until the **police** (pə lēs′) came. The man grumbled as they took him to jail.

21. What did the man stumble on? ______________________________

____

____

22. Name the three people who held the robber. ______________________________

____

____

Name ______________________________

Teacher's Initials ______

Worksheet 48
Phonics Intervention
ph

Coding and Reading

1. g r a p h
2. p h a s e
3. p h o n e
4. p h r a s e
5. t r a m p l e
6. r u f f l e s
7. c a b l e
8. t a c k l e
9. h e l p l e s s
10. a b s o r b

Spelling

11. ______________
12. ______________
13. ______________
14. ______________
15. ______________

Vocabulary

16. ______________
17. ______________
18. ______________
19. ______________

Alphabetizing

20. walk ______________ young

Reading Comprehension

(Worksheet 48, continued)

On a whim, I took my little sister to the zoo. She wanted to see the snakes first. The snakes squirmed when she tapped on the glass. Thinking the snakes could get loose, she jumped back and stepped on my toes. Next, my sister wanted to see the seals. When we got there, the seals splashed us as they dove into the clear blue pool. My sister screamed with glee and jumped into my lap. Then I took her to see a lynx. The lynx raised its foot in the air, and my sister jumped back again and hit my legs. I fell and landed in the mud. **All** (ŏl) in all, my sister **thought** (thŏt) that I was the best thing to see at the zoo.

21. What did my sister do that made the snakes squirm? ______________________

____

____

22. Why did my sister scream? ______________________________

____

____

Name ______________________________

Teacher's Initials ______

Worksheet 49
Phonics Intervention
Sight Words, 6

Sight Word Review

1. ______________
2. ______________
3. ______________
4. ______________
5. ______________
6. ______________
7. ______________
8. ______________
9. ______________
10. ______________

New Sight Words

11. early
12. women
13. woman
14. heard
15. earth
16. two
17. country
18. whose
19. fought
20. eye

Sentence Completion

(Worksheet 49, continued)

country early earth eye fought
heard two whose woman women

21. Those three ______________ are part of the cast in the play *Grease.*

22. Many years **ago** (ə gō′) people learned that the ____________ was not flat.

23. If I add three apples to __________ apples, I should get five apples.

24. My father ____________ a scream and came running to my room.

25. Quinn **bought** (bŏt) a horse and put it in a paddock in the ______________.

26. We should leave ___________ because I need to work on my math homework.

27. "______________ friend is at the door ringing the doorbell?" asked my mother.

28. We _____________ hard to be able to eat snacks in school.

29. My brother had sand in his __________ and he looked like he was crying.

30. The ______________ at the back of the bus is helping people with their bags.

Name ______________________________

Teacher's Initials ______

Worksheet 50
Phonics Intervention
Spelling with Final *ke* and *ve*

Spelling, Coding, and Reading

Spelling with *ck*, *k*, and *ke*

When spelling the final /k/ sound:
ck is found after a short vowel;
k is found after a consonant or a vowel digraph;
ke is found after a long vowel.

Spelling with *v* and *ve*

Spell the final /v/ sound with *ve*.
Spell the /v/ sound in any other position with *v*.

1. b r ǐ s ___
2. c h ō ___
3. c ā ___
4. l ā ___
5. w h ǐ s ___
6. s m ŏ ___
7. ___ e e n
8. m ǐ l ___
9. ___ ă n ' t
10. d ŭ s ___
11. d r i ___
12. v e l ___ e t
13. v a l ___
14. s o l ___
15. ___ o l l e y
16. s t o ___
17. ___ a n e
18. s l e e ___
19. l e a ___
20. s t r i ___

Name ______________________________

Teacher's Initials ______

Worksheet 51
Phonics Intervention
ēa̸, ĕa̸, e̸ā

LESSON WORKSHEETS

Coding and Reading

1. speak
2. death
3. great
4. squeaking
5. threat
6. treat
7. deaf
8. break
9. sly
10. tremble

Spelling

11. ______________
12. ______________
13. ______________
14. ______________
15. ______________

Vocabulary

16. ______________
17. ______________
18. ______________
19. ______________

Alphabetizing

20. chomp chin chap

____

____

____

Reading Comprehension

Last year we went to the beach and had a great time. It was a dream for me because I had been wanting to go there for so long. We got up early and fed bread to the sea gulls and then looked at the waves breaking against the shore as we basked in the sun. When we got too warm, we dove into the waves and swam like seals. We screamed when fish swam close by and squealed if they hit us. I was sad when we had to leave and tears ran off my cheeks. I want to go back to the beach when I have kids and teach them to sneak up on the waves and squeal at the fish.

21. What did we feed the sea gulls? ______________________________

____

____

22. When did we squeal? ______________________________

____

____

Name ______________________________

Teacher's Initials ______

Worksheet 52
Phonics Intervention
ẏ, -[y]

Coding and Reading

1. fifty
2. wealthy
3. forty
4. leaky
5. flimsy
6. guppy
7. enzyme
8. razzle
9. sneer
10. yoke

Spelling

11. ______________
12. ______________
13. ______________
14. ______________
15. ______________

Vocabulary

16. ______________
17. ______________
18. ______________
19. ______________

Alphabetizing

20. cling clang clung

____

____

____

Reading Comprehension

My sister has many, many fish. She started with one guppy and then added four more. In nine weeks she had twenty fish, and in six more weeks she had fifty. My mother and father think she should give some of her fish to her little brother, but my sister does not think I could take care of them as well as she does. I think she should do something too, or soon we will have fish in the bathtubs and maybe the sinks. My sister thinks that would be nifty.

21. What kind of fish was the girl's first fish? ____________________

____

____

22. Is she upset that she has so many fish? ____________________

____

____

Name ____________________________

Teacher's Initials ______

Worksheet 53
Phonics Intervention
gn, kn, wr

Coding and Reading

1. gnash
2. wriggle
3. knob
4. gnome
5. kneel
6. wren
7. dainty
8. healthy
9. teach
10. school

Spelling

11. ______________
12. ______________
13. ______________
14. ______________
15. ______________

Vocabulary

16. ______________
17. ______________
18. ______________
19. ______________

Alphabetizing

20. frost fresh frill

____

____

____

Reading Comprehension

(Worksheet 53, continued)

My mother likes to write. Last year she wrote some health fact sheets for doctors. Wrists, knees, and knuckles were her best subjects. Her fact sheets helped doctors learn **new** (nū) facts that they may not have **known** (nōn). My mother likes to read and write lessons for us too. Her lessons are fun because we get to do things like try to make bird nests the same way birds do. Next year my mother plans to write a craft book to teach others to knit and to make wreaths. I am so glad that my mother likes to write. I **love** (lŭv) to read her books!

21. What were my mom's best subjects? ____________________

____

____

22. Why do I like for my mom to write? ____________________

____

____

Name ______________________________

Teacher's Initials ______

Coding and Reading

1. a c e

2. t r a c e

3. a c c e n t

4. a d v i c e

5. c i r c l e

6. c e a s e

7. m e r c y

8. p a r c e l

9. c e l l a r

10. w r e a t h

Spelling

11. ______________

12. ______________

13. ______________

14. ______________

15. ______________

Vocabulary

16. ______________

17. ______________

18. ______________

19. ______________

Alphabetizing

20. lock long loft

____

____

____

Reading Comprehension

My sister, Cindy, and my brother, Lance, had to help me clear some space in the attic. It was quite a chore because we keep many things there. Lance wanted to keep a brace that my dad wore on his knee when he played soccer. My dad is fifty, and he played soccer when he was fifteen! Cindy wanted to keep my mom's dance **shoes** (shooz). My mom has not danced in thirty years! My brother and sister would not accept my advice to get rid of the old things. They just took the brace and shoes and put them in the cellar. I am sure I will get to clean the cellar next week!

21. What did Lance want to keep? ______________________________

____

____

22. Why did the speaker not want her brother and sister to store things in the cellar?

____

____

____

Name ____

Teacher's Initials ______

Worksheet 55
Phonics Intervention
Sight Words, 7

Sight Word Review

1. ________________
2. ________________
3. ________________
4. ________________
5. ________________
6. ________________
7. ________________
8. ________________
9. ________________
10. ________________

New Sight Words

11. gone
12. once
13. listen
14. mountain
15. half
16. guess (guest)
17. cousin
18. laugh
19. island
20. guard

Reading Comprehension

(Worksheet 55, continued)

My cousin Nancy has a fancy home on the top of a mountain in the middle of an island. She has a guard who lives at the top of the mountain and lets guests enter and leave the gate to her home. The guard has five guard dogs to help him. Nancy is gone half the time, so the guard has little to do. Once Nancy heard him chatting to the dogs when there was no one waiting to enter the gate. When the guard looked at Nancy, they both started to laugh.

21. Where is Nancy's home? ______________________________

____

____

22. What does the word "chatting" mean? ______________________________

____

____

Name ______________________________

Teacher's Initials ______

Worksheet 56
Phonics Intervention
ou, øū

Coding and Reading

1. bout
2. discount
3. noun
4. youth
5. douse
6. group
7. ulcer
8. knee
9. feast
10. grapple

Spelling

11. ________________
12. ________________
13. ________________
14. ________________
15. ________________

Vocabulary

16. ________________
17. ________________
18. ________________
19. ________________

Alphabetizing

20. fan far fat

____

fancy ________________

____

fast ________________

____

Reading Comprehension

(Worksheet 56, continued)

Once we woke up early to find fog outside. It looked like pea soup had settled on the ground. My hound dog, Lou, crouched as he struggled to walk from his house to his food. He seemed to want to go under the fog. When Lou found his food, he ate as fast as he could. I shouted to him, and he raised his head, squinting to see me. He made his way to the house, and when he found me, he leaped up at me. His snout hit my mouth, and I fell off the porch. I was not grouchy and did not shout as Lou landed in my lap. We **wrestled** (rĕs′ əld) on the ground and he doused me with mud.

21. Who squinted? ______________________________

____

____

22. What hit my mouth? ______________________________

____

____

Name ______________________

Teacher's Initials ______

Worksheet 57
Phonics Intervention

ow, ōw

Coding and Reading

1. stow
2. row
3. howl
4. scowl
5. willow
6. minnow
7. down
8. cinch
9. rainbow
10. slouch

Spelling

11. ______
12. ______
13. ______
14. ______
15. ______

Vocabulary

16. ______
17. ______
18. ______
19. ______

Alphabetizing

20. ruffle run rude

rubble

______

______

rule

______

Reading Comprehension

"I know! Let's go camping!" shouted Clay.

"Wow! That sounds good to me," said Willow.

"Where should we go?" Clay asked.

"I think we should go down to the lake where we can swim and ride boats," said Willow.

"**Oh** (ō), I don't want to go swimming or boating. I want to get up at five, set out trot lines, and fish until the sun goes down," frowned Clay.

"I think your concept of camping is not the same as mine," scowled Willow. "Maybe we should just stay in town and clean house."

21. Who wants to go swimming and boating? ____________________

____

____

22. What does Clay want to do? ____________________

____

____

Name ______________________________

Teacher's Initials ______

Worksheet 58
Phonics Intervention
oi, oy

Coding and Reading

1. b r o i l
2. h o i s t
3. p l o y
4. c o i l
5. f o u l
6. c o w b o y
7. t o i l
8. f r o w n
9. e l b o w
10. a b l e

Spelling

11. ____________
12. ____________
13. ____________
14. ____________
15. ____________

Vocabulary

16. ____________
17. ____________
18. ____________
19. ____________

Alphabetizing

20. swim sword swarm

____

sweat

____

____

swung

Reading Comprehension

Cassy enjoyed going on long walks. One day she found a coin sitting in oil in the middle of the road. The coin was old and quite tarnished, so Cassy took it home and cleaned it up. Then she took it to a woman in town who was known for finding and keeping old coins. The woman told Cassy that her coin was quite old and worth a lot. Cassy was filled with joy to know that she had found a rare coin. She took it to her room to keep until she could find out how much it was worth.

21. Where did Cassy find the old coin? ______________________________

____

____

22. What did she do with it? ______________________________

____

____

Name ______________________________

Teacher's Initials ______

Worksheet 59
Phonics Intervention
vc|cvc|cv

Coding and Reading

1. absentee
2. Atlantic
3. establish
4. embargo
5. fantastic
6. moist
7. how
8. low
9. you
10. trout

Spelling

11. ______________
12. ______________
13. ______________
14. ______________
15. ______________

Vocabulary

16. ______________
17. ______________
18. ______________
19. ______________

Alphabetizing

20. brick bread brush

brace______________

____

____

broke______________

____

Reading Comprehension

(Worksheet 59, continued)

Last year, my cousin Lesley and I went on a trip to the state of Vermont. We stayed in a little town named Randolph. While we were there, we learned many facts **about** (ə bowt′) the state. Vermont is a **small** (smŏl) state on the eastern side of the U.S.; it ranks 43rd in size of **all** (ŏl) the states. The Atlantic Ocean is to the east of Vermont. The state bird is the hermit thrush, and the state song is "Hail, Vermont." One state fish is the brook trout. Fort Dummer, one of the first **settlements** (set′ əl mənts) in Vermont, was established in 1724 to help keep people safe from French raids. Vermont is pretty in September when the leaves start to turn yellow and red. Vermont is a fantastic place to see!

21. Where did Lesley and I stay? ____________________

____

____

22. Why was Fort Dummer established? ____________________

____

____

Name ____________________

Teacher's Initials ______

Doubling Rule

To begin, make:

1 check mark if a root word ends with **one** vowel and **one** consonant.
1 check mark if a suffix is a **vowel suffix.**

When finished:

If you have **2** check marks, **double the final consonant** before adding the suffix.
If you have **fewer than 2** check marks, just **add the suffix.**

Example: ☑ stop + ☑ ed = **stopped**

1. ☐ sob + ☐ ing = ____________

2. ☐ pass + ☐ ed = ____________

3. ☐ hat + ☐ less = ____________

4. ☐ seat + ☐ ed = ____________

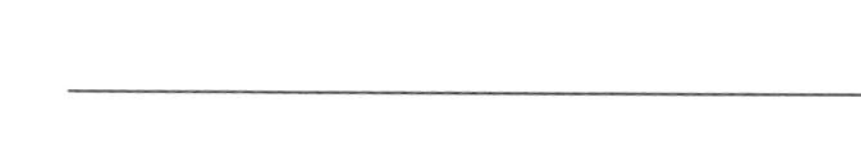

5. ☐ slop + ☐ y = ____________

6. ☐ seek + ☐ ing = ____________

7. ☐ sad + ☐ est = ____________

8. ☐ mist + ☐ y = ____________

Name ____

Teacher's Initials ______

Worksheet 61
Phonics Intervention
Sight Words, 8

Sight Word Review

1. ____________________
2. ____________________
3. ____________________
4. ____________________
5. ____________________
6. ____________________
7. ____________________
8. ____________________
9. ____________________
10. ____________________

New Sight Words

11. rough
12. thought
13. cough
14. tough
15. bought
16. done
17. through
18. though
19. busy
20. brought

Reading Comprehension

Shelly had a tough day. Her mother had a bad cough, so Shelly thought it would be nice if she took her two-year-old brother, Jay, to work with her. Shelly's job involves feeding the dogs at the **animal** (ăn′ ə məl) shelter. It would not have been so bad if Jay had not brought his kitten. Shelly had bought some dog food and was busy dishing it out when Jay's kitten got loose and started to run through the dog pens. It was pure **chaos** (kā′ ŏs) as the dogs ran after the kitten and made Shelly spill the food. She cleaned up the mess and fed the dogs. Though Shelly had a rough day, at least her work was done.

21. Where does Shelly work? ______________________________

____

____

22. What does "chaos" mean?

○ Good feelings
○ A mess; **confusion** (kən fū′ zhŭn)
○ Sad feelings

23. The best title for this tale would be:

○ Shelly's Bad Cough
○ Dogs + Kitten = Chaos
○ Jay and the Dog Food

Name ____________________

Teacher's Initials ______

Worksheet 62
Phonics Intervention
vc|ccv and vcc|cv

Coding and Reading

1. a n t h e m
2. b u r g l a r
3. d i s t r i c t
4. d o l p h i n
5. e m p l o y
6. i n s t a n t
7. m e r c h a n t
8. o i n t m e n t
9. w o r s h i p
10. i n s t e a d

Spelling

11. ____________
12. ____________
13. ____________
14. ____________
15. ____________

Vocabulary

16. ____________
17. ____________
18. ____________
19. ____________

Alphabetizing

20. bask be babble blurry bleach

____

____

____

____

____

Sentence Completion

(Worksheet 62, continued)

anthem burglar district dolphin employ
instant merchant ointment worship instead

21. A ______________ is a little whale and is known by some to be quite **intelligent** (ĭn tĕl′ ə jənt).

22. Kelly chose the purple dress ______________ of the blue one.

23. Our school ______________ has a strict dress code **policy** (pŏl′ ə sē).

24. The **national** (nă′ shə nəl) ______________ is going to be sung by my cousin at the soccer game.

25. Please put some ______________ on the burn to **prevent** (prĭ vĕnt′) it from hurting.

Name ____________________

Teacher's Initials ______

Worksheet 63
Phonics Intervention

Spelling with Final, Stable Syllables

Spelling, Coding, and Reading

1. ____________
2. ____________
3. ____________
4. ____________
5. ____________
6. ____________
7. ____________
8. ____________
9. ____________
10. ____________

Spelling

11. ____________
12. ____________
13. ____________
14. ____________
15. ____________

Vocabulary

16. ____________
17. ____________
18. ____________
19. ____________

Alphabetizing

20. cash check chains cinch camp

____

____

____

____

____

Reading Comprehension

(Worksheet 63, continued)

A storm system was heading our way. Our dog trembled when the thunder rumbled and the sky lit up. The maple tree at the back of our house swayed back and forth as the wind increased. I struggled to grab the chairs so they would not blow into our swimming pool. As the wind got stronger, little pebbles were picked up and thrown; they stung as they hit our ankles. As my son ran into the house, I could hear him mumble that he **hoped** (hōpt) the cable didn't go out since he wanted to see a game on T.V.

21. Who trembled? ______________________________

____

____

22. Why did the son want the cable T.V. to work?

- ○ So he could see a game on T.V.
- ○ So he could play chess
- ○ So his mom would be happy

23. What swayed back and forth?

- ○ The house
- ○ The swimming pool
- ○ The maple tree

Name ____________________

Teacher's Initials ______

Worksheet 64
Phonics Intervention
ġ

Coding and Reading

1. gem
2. gypsum
3. suggest
4. passenger
5. urgent
6. gentle
7. gerbil
8. gentry
9. gist
10. gender

Spelling

11. ____________
12. ____________
13. ____________
14. ____________
15. ____________

Vocabulary

16. ____________
17. ____________
18. ____________
19. ____________

Alphabetizing

20. warm whimper wheel wild week

____

____

____

____

____

Reading Comprehension

I have a friend, Gene, who has two gerbils. If you hold them **gingerly** (jĭn′ jer lē), they will not bite. One has a short, thick tail, and the other has a longer tail. Their fur is so soft! The gerbils are **small** (smŏl) now, but they will soon grow larger. Gene is leaving on an urgent trip to Houston and asked me to keep his gerbils since I am his friend. I asked my mom if I could take care of them for Gene. She said yes, so I will keep them next week. We don't know the gerbils' genders yet, but I hope that some day they have little gerbils, and maybe Gene will sell them, if you get my gist.

21. Where is Gene going? ______________________________

____

____

22. What is the gist of the speaker's comment?

- ○ He wants a gerbil for his mom.
- ○ He does not like gerbils.
- ○ He would like to have a gerbil of his own.

23. In sentence two, the word "gingerly" must mean __________ .

- ○ To squeeze the gerbils
- ○ To handle them **carefully** (kăr′ fəl ē)
- ○ To hold their mouths closed

Name ______________________________

Teacher's Initials ______

Worksheet 65
Phonics Intervention
v́|cv

Coding and Reading

1. bonus
2. basic
3. fever
4. duty
5. tripod
6. unit
7. agent
8. parsley
9. fizzle
10. swoon

Spelling

11. ______________
12. ______________
13. ______________
14. ______________
15. ______________

Vocabulary

16. ______________
17. ______________
18. ______________
19. ______________

Alphabetizing

20. huddle hobble hi he hush

____

____

____

____

____

Reading Comprehension

(Worksheet 65, continued)

My dog, Jip, an Irish Setter, had a crazy day! First, he woke up when the baby started sobbing. He came into the house to see if he could help but instead found some gravy that had spilled and started to eat it. Mom did not see Jip and tripped over him, cutting her chin open.

We rushed her to town and left Jip in the house. He scattered my music books in the den, gorged himself on **all** (ŏl) the snacks on the counter, broke my brother's toy robot, and knocked my dad's tripod into my mom's old basin on the table. He scattered stuff in all the rooms.

When the crisis was over, we returned home and made Jip leave the house until later. For a long time, I will not forget the moment when we walked into the house and found Jip's mess!

21. What kind of dog is Jip? ______________________________

____

____

22. What does "gorged" mean?

○ To eat lots of food
○ To get dirty
○ To get hurt

23. The best title for this tale would be __________ .

○ Mom Goes Shopping
○ The Lost Dog
○ Jip's Day in the House

24. Name three things Jip did while he was in the house. ______________________________

____

____

Name ______________________________

Teacher's Initials ______

Worksheet 66

Phonics Intervention

-**let**, -**ly**

Coding and Reading

1. leaflet
2. wristlet
3. starlet
4. likely
5. mostly
6. centrally
7. urgently
8. richer
9. softest
10. stringy

Spelling

11. ________________
12. ________________
13. ________________
14. ________________
15. ________________

Vocabulary

16. ________________
17. ________________
18. ________________
19. ________________

Alphabetizing

20. squeak smock scuff sway scorch

____

____

____

____

____

Reading Comprehension

(Worksheet 66, continued)

We had a contest at our school. Our goal was to find the shortest girl and the strongest boy. We quickly found that Jenny, the girl with a purple wristlet on her arm, was the shortest girl after we had her stand by each of the other girls. Miss Rankin jotted down Jenny's name in a booklet on her desk. Jenny was lucky to be a short person that day.

The strongest boy was harder to find. We had each boy lift as many books as he could until one boy, Kitt, lifted more books than any of the other boys. You could see Kitt's pride in his huge smile. He told Miss Rankin that he would lug books to her car if she needed help some day. She said that she would gladly accept his offer.

It was a fun day and a nice break since we didn't have to do as much work in class.

21. Who was the shortest girl? ______________________________

____

____

22. What did Kitt do to show he was the strongest?

- ○ He picked up a car.
- ○ He lifted the most books.
- ○ He took Miss Rankin's books to her car.

23. In this passage, the word "lug" must mean ____________ .

- ○ To carry
- ○ To throw
- ○ To push in a cart

24. Where did Miss Rankin jot down the names of the students? ________________

____

____

Name ______________________________

Teacher's Initials ______

Worksheet 67
Phonics Intervention
Sight Words, 9

Sight Word Review

1. ________________
2. ________________
3. ________________
4. ________________
5. ________________
6. ________________
7. ________________
8. ________________
9. ________________
10. ________________

New Sight Words

11. tastes
12. sign
13. shoe
14. push
15. often
16. move
17. very
18. floor
19. climb
20. certain

Sentence Completion

(Worksheet 67, continued)

certain climb floor move often
push shoe sign tastes very

21. "Please do not walk on my clean ____________ while your shoes are muddy!" begged Mom.

22. After my uncle ate the rattlesnake, he said, "It ______________ like **chicken** (chĭk′ ən)."

23. ____________ the button and see if the bell rings so we will know if it is working.

24. I am not ______________ if the meeting is at three or at five.

25. It is not ____________ that you get a warm, sunny day in the middle of winter.

26. Please ____________ the plant off the table so I can set the bags of food there.

27. I am missing one ____________, and if I don't find it, the other will not be of any use.

28. Let's ____________ the mountain to see what is on the other side.

29. My mother said that she was ___________ impressed with my grades this year!

30. The ___________ said, "If you can read this, you are following too closely."

Name ______________________________

Teacher's Initials ______

Worksheet 68
Phonics Intervention
igh

Coding and Reading

1. blight
2. thigh
3. fright
4. sigh
5. slight
6. plight
7. cedar
8. focus
9. slogan
10. wildest

Spelling

11. ______________
12. ______________
13. ______________
14. ______________
15. ______________

Vocabulary

16. ______________
17. ______________
18. ______________
19. ______________

Alphabetizing

20. hassle ______________ kneel

Reading Comprehension

(Worksheet 68, continued)

One night as friends Kiley and Toby were peering at the dark night, a bright streak of light flashed in the sky. "It might have been a shooting star," said Kiley. "That's right," said Toby. "A shooting star is the streak of light formed as fragments from space heat up and turn to vapor as they enter the earth's **atmosphere** (ăt′ mə sfēr)." "Wow," said Kiley, "I didn't know that! I just like to see the streak of light and make a wish. I have been told that if you make a wish on a shooting star, it might come true." "Kiley, what wish would you make?" asked Toby. "Well," said Kiley, "my wish would be to make an A on my test in the morning." "You know what I suggest?" asked Toby. "I suggest that you read the chapter **before** (bĭ for′) you take the test. I don't think even shooting stars can help you make A's on tests."

21. What does a shooting star look like? ______________________________

____

____

22. When shooting stars enter the earth's atmosphere they turn into __________.

○ Vapor

○ Clouds

○ Rain

23. What had Kiley been told **about** (ə bowt′) shooting stars?

○ They will help you make A's.

○ If you make a wish on one, it might come true.

○ They are stars that shoot moon dust at each other.

24. What was Toby's advice?

○ Wish on a star to get an A.

○ Read the chapter and then take the test.

○ Take the test later.

Name ______________________________

Teacher's Initials ______

Worksheet 69
Phonics Intervention
tch

Coding and Reading

1. thatch
2. blotch
3. sketch
4. twitch
5. clutch
6. etch
7. notch
8. flight
9. gravy
10. acrid

Spelling

11. ____________________
12. ____________________
13. ____________________
14. ____________________
15. ____________________

Vocabulary

16. ____________________
17. ____________________
18. ____________________
19. ____________________

Alphabetizing

20. douse ____________________ embargo

Reading Comprehension

(Worksheet 69, continued)

Matt and Mitch play *Hide and Go Seek* with their friends on Sunday nights. Each child runs and hides while Mitch counts to twenty. When Mitch gets to twenty, he tries to find the other children. Many of them hide in the woods by the school.

In the summer, the boys often hide in a deep ditch that is infested with chiggers, or harvest mites. When they get home after the game, they sometimes find that their skin is **covered** (kəv′ erd) with little red lumps. The itch from the bite of a chigger comes later when a rash known as scrub itch breaks out on the skin. A tiny, scarlet mite can be seen in the center of most of the lumps.

Matt and Mitch spend the next **few** (fū) weeks itching and scratching. It's lucky that the boys enjoy the game so much or they would not risk getting infested with chiggers each summer.

21. When do Matt and Mitch play *Hide and Go Seek*? ______________________________

____

____

22. **Another** (ə nəth′ ər) name for chiggers is what? ______________________________

____

____

23. In this tale, "infested" means ____________ .

○ Grassy
○ Itchy
○ Filled with

24. Why are chiggers such a problem?

○ They don't survive in winter.
○ They **cause** (kŏz) an itchy rash.
○ Only boys get chiggers.

25. Why do you think that the boys keep playing even when they know the chiggers will bite them? ____

____

____

Name ______________________________

Teacher's Initials ______

Worksheet 70
Phonics Intervention
dge

Coding and Reading

1. budge
2. wedge
3. lodge
4. ridge
5. badge
6. sludge
7. splotch
8. bright
9. fiber
10. challenge

Spelling

11. ______________
12. ______________
13. ______________
14. ______________
15. ______________

Vocabulary

16. ______________
17. ______________
18. ______________
19. ______________

Alphabetizing

20. sobbing ______________ stow

Reading Comprehension

It was a cold, snowy night. Madge and I were heading into town to see our friend and to take her some freshly made fudge. We came up over a ridge and found a car stranded on an icy bridge. It was hard to judge how close the car was to the edge, but it looked as if even a slight nudge might push it over into the creek.

A woman with a badge drove up after us, trying to keep from hitting the tree near the road. She went right to work, putting a wedge under the rear tire to keep the car from slipping off the bridge. Then we pushed to get the car off the edge of the bridge. At first it would not budge, but soon the car slid into a safe spot.

We shook hands and the woman left. I jumped into my car and found an oily smudge on my face. A clean cloth took care of the smudge. I was **cautious** (kŏʹ shəs) as I drove over the bridge and on into town. We could not wait to tell our friend the tale of the car on the bridge.

21. What was the **weather** (wĕthʹ er) like in this tale? ______________________

____

____

22. What did Madge and the speaker have for their friend? ______________________

____

____

23. What did the woman with a badge put under the tire?

○ A wedge
○ Chunks of fudge
○ A tree

24. Choose the correct order of **events** (ē vĕntsʹ).

○ Pushed the car, put a wedge under the rear tire, shook hands
○ Put a wedge under the rear tire, pushed the car, shook hands
○ Cleaned the smudge, pushed the car, made fudge
○ Shook hands, drove over the bridge, pushed the car

25. A good title for this tale might be ____________ .

○ The Night We Slid Off A Bridge
○ An Icy Rescue
○ How to Freeze Fudge

Name ______________________________

Teacher's Initials ______

Worksheet 71
Phonics Intervention
Spelling with Final *dge* and *ge*

Spelling with *dge* and *ge*

When spelling the final /j/ sound:
dge is found after a short vowel;
ge is found after anything else.

Spelling, Coding, and Reading

1. ______________
2. ______________
3. ______________
4. ______________
5. ______________
6. ______________
7. ______________
8. ______________
9. ______________
10. ______________

Spelling

11. ______________
12. ______________
13. ______________
14. ______________
15. ______________

Vocabulary

16. ______________
17. ______________
18. ______________
19. ______________

Alphabetizing

20. shirk ______________ stumps

Name ________________________________

Teacher's Initials ______

Worksheet 72
Phonics Intervention
Spelling with Final *ch* and *tch*

Spelling with *ch* and *tch*

When spelling the final /ch/ sound:
tch is found after a short vowel;
ch is found after anything else.

Spelling, Coding, and Reading

1. ____________________

2. ____________________

3. ____________________

4. ____________________

5. ____________________

6. ____________________

7. ____________________

8. ____________________

9. ____________________

10. ____________________

Spelling

11. ____________________

12. ____________________

13. ____________________

14. ____________________

15. ____________________

Vocabulary

16. ____________________

17. ____________________

18. ____________________

19. ____________________

Alphabetizing

20. sifting ____________________ solve

Name ______________________________

Teacher's Initials ______

Worksheet 73
Phonics Intervention
Sight Words, 10

Sight Word Review

1. ________________
2. ________________
3. ________________
4. ________________
5. ________________
6. ________________
7. ________________
8. ________________
9. ________________
10. ________________

New Sight Words

11. nothing
12. build
13. none
14. heart
15. answer
16. straight
17. clothes
18. February
19. above
20. caught (taught)

Sentence Completion

(Worksheet 73, continued)

above	answer	build	caught	clothes
February	heart	none	nothing	straight

21. My dad taught me to stand ______________ and hold my head high.

22. They ______________ the person who broke into the store and stole the coats and pants.

23. **Valentine's** (văl′ ən tīnz) Day is in ______________, and Thanksgiving is in November.

24. The child said she didn't know the ______________ to number six, but she could answer number ten.

25. ______________ of the girls who came to try out for the part had red hair.

26. For Valentine's Day we made a cake that looked like a huge ______________ and gave it to our teacher.

27. Let's ______________ a **castle** (kăs′ əl) in the sand and then let the waves topple it.

28. Put my ______________ in the dryer so they will be dry when I get back.

29. No one should think that he or she is ______________ the **laws** (lôz) of the land.

30. There is ______________ that tastes as good to me as fudge.

Name ____

Teacher's Initials _____

Worksheet 74
Phonics Intervention
´[tion

Coding and Reading

1. action
2. caption
3. carnation
4. dictation
5. exception
6. foundation
7. friction
8. fractions
9. interruption
10. motion

Spelling

11. ____________________
12. ____________________
13. ____________________
14. ____________________
15. ____________________

Vocabulary

16. ____________________
17. ____________________
18. ____________________
19. ____________________

Alphabetizing

20. ________ nothing
________ straight
________ caught
________ clothes
________ build
________ heart

Reading Comprehension

(Worksheet 74, continued)

The **National** Anthem

Can you answer this question? What song starts with the words "**Oh,** say can you see, by the **dawn's** early light!"? That is the first line of this country's national anthem. An anthem is a song of praise. This country's anthem is *The Star-Spangled Banner*. It tells the tale of a battle that was fought in 1814. The action of battle went on through the day and through the night. In the dark of night, the flag could only be seen by the red glare of rockets. At morning's light, the flag was still flying. A man named Francis Scott Key was at this battle. When Key caught sight of the flag, he was so happy that he started to write **about** it. His words were put to **music.** People in the U.S. heard the song, and the words filled them with pride in their flag and their country. In 1931, Congress made this song our national anthem. This song reminds us that we live in "the land of the free and the home of the brave."

21. What kind of song is an anthem? ______________________________

____

____

22. When did Congress make *The Star-Spangled Banner* our national anthem? __________

____

____

23. What does *The Star-Spangled Banner* tell the tale of?

- ○ It tells the tale of a battle.
- ○ It tells the tale of Francis Scott Key's life.
- ○ It tells a tale of rockets.
- ○ None of the above

24. When did Francis Scott Key write *The Star-Spangled Banner?*

- ○ 1931
- ○ 1941
- ○ 1841
- ○ None of the above

25. How did the national anthem make the people of this country feel when they heard it?

- ○ Filled with pride
- ○ Very sad
- ○ Very mad
- ○ None of the above

national: nash′ ən əl	**oh:** ō	**dawn's:** dŏnz	**about:** ə bowt′	**music:** mū′ zĭk

LESSON WORKSHEETS

Name ______________________________

Teacher's Initials ______

Worksheet 75
Phonics Intervention
vc´|v

Coding and Reading

1. cabin
2. comics
3. city
4. denim
5. sliver
6. pleasant
7. starvation
8. chronic
9. coupon
10. meadow

Spelling

11. ____________________
12. ____________________
13. ____________________
14. ____________________
15. ____________________

Vocabulary

16. ____________________
17. ____________________
18. ____________________
19. ____________________

Alphabetizing

20. __________ should

__________ some

__________ sign

__________ shoe

__________ sugar

__________ sure

Reading Comprehension

(Worksheet 75, continued)

Martin Luther King, Jr. Day

Once there were **laws** in parts of this country that did not permit black people to sit with, eat with, or go to school with white people. In some states they could not even vote. Martin Luther King, Jr. was a black man who helped to change these laws. He was born in Atlanta, **Georgia,** on **January** 15, 1929. His father was a preacher. Martin would grow up to be a preacher too. He would tell people not to shop in any store where they did not get **equal** rights. He would tell them not to ride on any bus where they could not sit in any seat. Many times Dr. King and those who followed him were put in jail. In 1963, Dr. King led a march on **Washington,** D.C. Two hundred thousand people came to hear him. Many more heard him on T.V. Dr. King spoke of his dream that one day people would be treated the same. In 1964, the U.S. Congress **voted** to grant everyone the same rights. This was the Civil Rights Act of 1964. It made some people very mad. One of those people shot and killed Martin Luther King, Jr. People were very sad. Congress voted to **honor** Dr. King and make his birthday a **holiday.** Now on January 15, Dr. King's birthday, we remember and honor this brave man.

21. Where was Martin Luther King, Jr. born? ____________________

____

22. What did Dr. King fight for? ____________________

____

23. How did Dr. King tell people to fight for their rights?

○ Ride on any bus.
○ Shop in any store.
○ Remember his birthday.
○ None of the above

24. What did Dr. King say in Washington, D.C., in 1963?

○ He said to shop in stores where treatment is not fair.
○ He spoke of his dream that one day everyone would be treated the same.
○ He said to ride on a bus where you cannot sit in any seat.
○ None of the above

25. How was Dr. King honored?

○ His birthday was made a holiday.
○ People heard him on T.V.
○ Many people heard him speak in Washington, D.C.
○ None of the above

laws: lŏz **Georgia:** jor′ jə **January:** jăn′ yə wĕr ē **equal:** ē′ kwəl
Washington: wŏsh′ ĭng tən **voted:** vōt′ əd **honor:** ŏn′ er **holiday:** hŏl′ ĭ dā

Name ______________________________

Teacher's Initials ______

Worksheet 76
Phonics Intervention
ä

Coding and Reading

1. waltz

2. swampy

3. squall

4. limit

5. call

6. malt

7. swallow

8. washer

9. disruption

10. swans

Spelling

11. ________________

12. ________________

13. ________________

14. ________________

15. ________________

Vocabulary

16. ________________

17. ________________

18. ________________

19. ________________

Alphabetizing

20. ________ graph

________ fable

________ rind

________ deaf

________ marsh

________ verb

Reading Comprehension

(Worksheet 76, continued)

The Right to Vote

The right to vote gives people a say in picking their leaders. It is a right that many people fought to get. At one time there were laws that did not allow women and black people to vote. In the 1800s, Susan B. **Anthony** fought to change these laws. In 1870, black men were granted the right to vote. In 1920, women were too. Some states made up rules that made it hard for black people to vote. Leaders like Martin Luther King, Jr. fought to change these rules. At last, in 1965, the U.S. Congress passed some laws that got rid of these unjust rules and that **protected** everyone's right to vote.

At one time you had to be 21 or older to vote, but in 1971, people 18 or older were granted the right to vote. Now the rules that permit people to vote are easy. You must be a **citizen** of this country, you must be 18 or older, and you must live in a state for 50 days or more to vote there. People who want to vote must show that they meet these rules. This is called "registering to vote." Once you do this, your name is entered on a list of people who can vote. The right to vote is one of the most important rights people have in this country. When you have this right, use it! On **Election** Day, cast your vote for the people you want to be your leaders.

21. When did women get the right to vote? ______________________

____

____

22. Who were some of the leaders who fought to change unjust **voting** laws?

- ○ Susan B. Anthony
- ○ Martin Luther King, Jr.
- ○ None of the above
- ○ Both of the above

23. How old must you be to vote?

- ○ 21 or older
- ○ 18 or older
- ○ It does not matter.
- ○ None of the above

24. Why is it important to vote?

- ○ It is easy.
- ○ It is right.
- ○ It is your way of picking your leaders.
- ○ None of the above

25. How long must you live in a state in order to vote there?

- ○ 50 days or more
- ○ 18 days or more
- ○ 21 days or more
- ○ None of the above

Anthony: ăn′ thə nē **protected:** prə tĕk′ tĕd **citizen:** sĭt′ ə zĕn
Election: ē lĕk′ shŭn **voting:** vōt′ ĭng

Name ____________________

Teacher's Initials ______

Worksheet 77
Phonics Intervention
v|cv´

Coding and Reading

1. eject
2. section
3. unite
4. below
5. promote
6. punish
7. proceed
8. circulate
9. release
10. erase

Spelling

11. ____________
12. ____________
13. ____________
14. ____________
15. ____________

Vocabulary

16. ____________
17. ____________
18. ____________
19. ____________

Alphabetizing

20. ________ there
________ though
________ tough
________ talk
________ to
________ two

Reading Comprehension

(Worksheet 77, continued)

The Fourth of July

The Fourth of July is an important day in this country. It is our country's birthday. On this day in 1776 our country was born. Before then, our country was part of England. We were under the rule of the king of England. In the 1600s, England sent people to settle this country. They built homes and farms, planted crops, and started lives in a **new** land. The land was called England's **American colonies.** The people who made their homes there were called **colonists.** As time passed, the colonists began to think that they did not want the king to rule them. Instead, they wanted their independence, or the right to rule themselves. They wanted to rebel against the king. In the summer of 1776, leaders of the colonists met to discuss the kind of country that they wanted. They decided to write a **Declaration of Independence** to send to the king. The declaration was finished on July 4, 1776. In it, the colonists told the king that they wanted to rule themselves. This made the king very mad. He sent an army to make the colonists stay part of England. The colonists fought and beat England. Today, we are a free country, and every July 4 we **celebrate** our birthday. We ring bells, set off fireworks, and take pride in the brave people who helped to make us free.

21. When did England send people to settle this country? ______________________________

____

22. What did the colonists want? ____

____

23. When did the colonists write the Declaration of Independence?

- ○ In the 1600s
- ○ Each July
- ○ In 1776
- ○ None of the above

24. What did the king do when he got the Declaration of Independence?

- ○ He sent an army to fight the colonists.
- ○ He set off fireworks.
- ○ He gave the colonists their independence.
- ○ None of the above

25. Why do we celebrate July 4?

- ○ We like the summer.
- ○ It is the birthday of the king of England.
- ○ It is our country's birthday.
- ○ None of the above

new: nū **American colonies:** ə mĕr´ ə kən kŏl´ ə nēz **colonists:** kŏl´ ə nəsts
Declaration of Independence: dĕk lə rā´ shən ŭv ĭn də pĕn´ dəns
celebrate: sĕl´ ə brāt

Name ______________________________

Teacher's Initials ______

Worksheet 78
Phonics Intervention
v|cv´

Coding and Reading

1. adapt
2. conviction
3. ahead
4. liver
5. anointed
6. alert
7. amaze
8. wallet
9. dilute
10. divide

Spelling

11. ______________
12. ______________
13. ______________
14. ______________
15. ______________

Vocabulary

16. ______________
17. ______________
18. ______________
19. ______________

Alphabetizing

20. ________ what
________ who
________ was
________ where
________ would
________ were

Reading Comprehension

(Worksheet 78, continued)

The American Flag

Some people call the American flag "The Stars and Stripes." Some call it "The Red, White, and Blue." Others call it "Old Glory." No matter what it is called, the flag is one of the most important symbols of this country. Remember that in 1776 we had to fight against England to become a free country. Our army needed a flag to fly into battle. The leaders of our country **decided** that the flag should be red, white, and blue. Red stands for **courage,** white for **purity,** and blue for **justice.** The 13 stripes stand for the 13 colonies that were part of this country when the fight against England began. At that time, our leaders decided to call each of the 13 colonies a state. They added 13 stars to the flag to stand for each state. Whenever a state joins our nation, a star is added to the flag. We now have 50 stars that stand for each state that is part of this nation. When you see our nation's flag fly by in a parade, salute the flag and remember what it means to us all—that we are many states joined together to form one nation.

21. What **color** in the flag stands for courage? ______________________________

____

____

22. How many stars are on our flag today? ______________________________

____

____

23. What color in the flag stands for justice?

- ○ Red
- ○ White
- ○ Blue
- ○ None of the above

24. What do the 50 stars on our flag stand for?

- ○ Each state in our nation
- ○ The stars in the sky
- ○ The 13 colonies
- ○ None of the above

25. What does the flag tell about this nation?

- ○ We are all joined together.
- ○ We like stars and stripes.
- ○ We like the colors red, white, and blue.
- ○ None of the above

decided: dĭ sīd′ ĕd **courage:** ker′ ĭj **purity:** pyur′ ə tē
justice: jŭs′ təs **color:** kəl′ er

Name ______________________________

Teacher's Initials _____

Worksheet 79
Phonics Intervention
Sight Words, 11

Sight Word Review

1. ________________
2. ________________
3. ________________
4. ________________
5. ________________
6. ________________
7. ________________
8. ________________
9. ________________
10. ________________

New Sight Words

11. prove
12. full
13. sugar
14. beautiful
15. stomach
16. shoulder
17. Dr.
18. special
19. poor
20. Mrs.

Sentence Completion

(Worksheet 79, continued)

beautiful Dr. full Mrs. poor
prove shoulder special stomach sugar

21. After my teacher, Miss Grantham, weds Tom Abbott, her name will be ____________ Abbott.

22. In **court** (kort) you have to ____________ the other person did what you say he or she did.

23. That candy has a lot of ____________ in it, and when I eat some, it makes me feel sick.

24. The word ____________ means "needy" or "lacking **money** (mŭn′ ē)."

25. The mountains were so ______________ we could hardly take our eyes off them.

26. We had to go to the doctor's office and see __________ Green to find out why our stomachs hurt.

27. My ______________ hurt because I ate too much candy!

28. Can you rub my left ______________, which is very sore?

29. I have now learned that when you feel __________, you should stop eating.

30. It is nice when someone makes you feel _____________ by saying nice things about you.

Name ______________________________

Teacher's Initials ______

Worksheet 80
Phonics Intervention
Dropping Rule

Dropping Rule

To begin, make:
- 1 check mark if the root word ends with a **silent *e*.**
- 1 check mark if the suffix is a **vowel suffix.**

When finished:
- If you have **2** check marks, **drop the silent *e*** before adding the suffix.
- If you have **fewer than 2** check marks, just **add the suffix.**

Example: ☑ brace + ☑ ed = **braced**

1. ☐ slide + ☐ ing = ____________
2. ☐ time + ☐ less = ____________
3. ☐ plate + ☐ s = ____________
4. ☐ tune + ☐ er = ____________
5. ☐ shade + ☐ y = ____________
6. ☐ peek + ☐ ing = ____________
7. ☐ file + ☐ ing = ____________
8. ☐ fight + ☐ er = ____________

Name ______________________________

Teacher's Initials ______

Worksheet 81
Phonics Intervention
au, aw

Coding and Reading

1. crawl
2. cause
3. straws
4. awful
5. scrawl
6. thaw
7. yawning
8. auction
9. outlaw
10. Austin

Spelling

11. ______________
12. ______________
13. ______________
14. ______________
15. ______________

Vocabulary

16. ______________
17. ______________
18. ______________
19. ______________

Alphabetizing

20. glare ______________ glide

Reading Comprehension

(Worksheet 81, continued)

President **George** Washington

There is one man who is known as the "Father of Our Country." This man is George Washington. George Washington was born on February 22, 1732. As a young man, he was a farmer, a **soldier,** and a leader of the colonies. Because he did not want to live under the laws of England, Washington led the army of the United States to victory against England in the cause of independence. When the war was over, many wanted to make Washington king. When he would not take that title, he was elected as the first president of the United States. Like the father of a baby, he helped the country begin to grow strong and wise.

Washington was president for 8 years. Then he went home to his farm, where he stayed until he died in 1799. This country **honors** Washington in many ways. His face is on stamps, on the dollar bill, and on the 25-cent coin. The **capital** of this nation is named for him. A special monument was built there in his honor. He is remembered as "first in war, first in peace, and first in the hearts of his countrymen."

21. When was George Washington born? ______________________________

____

____

22. How long was he president? ______________________________

____

____

23. How did this country honor George Washington?

- ○ It made him king.
- ○ It named the capital for him.
- ○ It gave him a farm.
- ○ None of the above

24. Why do you think Washington is called the "Father of Our Country"?

- ○ He treated his army as if they were kings.
- ○ He helped the country begin to grow strong and wise.
- ○ He told Americans what to do.
- ○ None of the above

25. What did Washington do when he stopped being president?

- ○ He fought a war with England.
- ○ He signed the Declaration of Independence.
- ○ He went home to his farm.
- ○ None of the above

George: jorj	**soldier:** sōl′ jer	**honors:** ŏn′ erz	**capital:** kăp′ ə təl

Name ______________________________

Teacher's Initials _____

Worksheet 82
Phonics Intervention

ew

LESSON WORKSHEETS

Coding and Reading

1. p e w
2. n e w
3. c r e w
4. f a u l t
5. k n e w
6. c h e w i n g
7. c u r f e w
8. c a s h e w s
9. l a w n
10. n e p h e w s

Spelling

11. ______________
12. ______________
13. ______________
14. ______________
15. ______________

Vocabulary

16. ______________
17. ______________
18. ______________
19. ______________

Alphabetizing

20. dusk ______________ dwell

Reading Comprehension

The Constitution of the United States

In 1783, the American army defeated the army of England. The American colonies were free. Now this nation had to make laws to rule itself. Leaders such as George Washington met to write these laws. The leaders drew up a constitution. A constitution states the laws of a nation. The Constitution of the United States sets out the rules of **government** that we follow. Our national government is divided into three parts: the **executive** branch, the **legislative** branch, and the **judicial** branch. The executive branch is headed by the president. This branch must make sure that the nation's laws are followed. The legislative branch is headed by Congress. It makes the laws. The judicial branch is headed by the **Supreme Court.** It interprets what the laws mean. Each branch acts as a check on the others. For example, Congress can make a law, but the president must sign it. If anyone thinks that a law is not right, he or she can go to the Supreme Court. The Court will decide if the law follows the rules of the Constitution. Since the Constitution was signed in 1787, its laws have ruled this country. As the nation changed and grew, so did the Constitution. Following the Constitution is how we keep this nation free.

21. When was the Constitution signed? ______________________________

____

____

22. What are the names of the three parts of the United States government? __________

____

____

23. What is the job of the executive branch?

- ○ To make the laws.
- ○ To make sure the laws are followed.
- ○ To tell what the laws mean.
- ○ None of the above

24. Which branch of government is headed by the Supreme Court?

- ○ Executive branch
- ○ Legislative branch
- ○ Judicial branch
- ○ None of the above

25. What is the Constitution for?

- ○ To divide the government
- ○ To set out the rules of government
- ○ To check on the three parts of government
- ○ To help the president sign laws

government: gəv′ ern mənt **executive:** ĭg zĕk′ yət ĭv **legislative:** lĕj′ ə slāt ĭv **judicial:** jū dĭsh′ əl **Supreme Court:** sə prēm′ kort

Name ______________________________

Teacher's Initials ______

Worksheet 83
Phonics Intervention
ə
o

Coding and Reading

1. w o n
2. t o n
3. d a w n
4. c o n f i r m i n g
5. c o m f o r t
6. c o m p l e t e
7. c o n s e r v e
8. d e w
9. p h a n t o m
10. j a u n t

Spelling

11. ______________
12. ______________
13. ______________
14. ______________
15. ______________

Vocabulary

16. ______________
17. ______________
18. ______________
19. ______________

Alphabetizing

20. little ______________ lobby

Reading Comprehension

(Worksheet 83, continued)

The Supreme Court

The Supreme Court of the United States is the highest court in the country. Its job is to make sure that all laws are fair and followed by everyone in the country. When a new law is passed, the Supreme Court can decide if it follows the Constitution. If it does not, the Court can order the law to be changed. The Supreme Court is made up of nine members. The head of the Court is the **chief justice.** The other members are called **justices.** Justices are picked by the president and must be **approved** by Congress. At one time the justices were all white men. In 1967, Thurgood Marshall was the first black man selected to serve on the Court. In 1981, Sandra Day O'Connor was the first woman appointed to the Court. The Supreme Court meets every year for about nine months. The Court does not consider every case that comes before it. It rules only on cases that the justices think are important to the whole country. Once the Supreme Court rules on something, it becomes the law of the land. When the Supreme Court speaks, everyone in the United States listens.

21. How many members are on the Supreme Court? ______________________

____

____

22. What are members of the Supreme Court called? ______________________

____

____

23. What is the job of the Supreme Court?

- ○ To make the laws
- ○ To make sure that our laws follow the Constitution
- ○ To consider every case that comes before it
- ○ None of the above

24. Who is the head of the Supreme Court?

- ○ The president
- ○ Congress
- ○ The chief justice
- ○ None of the above

25. What happens once the Supreme Court rules on a law?

- ○ People can decide if they want to follow the law.
- ○ Congress must approve the law.
- ○ The president must approve the law.
- ○ None of the above

chief justice: chēf jŭs′ təs **justices:** jŭs′ təs əz **approved:** ə prūvd′

Name ______________________________

Teacher's Initials _____

Worksheet 84

Phonics Intervention

ei, ēi̸, īe̸, i̸ē

Coding and Reading

1. d i e
2. p a u s e
3. b r i e f
4. s l a w
5. f i e r c e
6. s h r i e k i n g
7. r e i n
8. f l e w
9. r e c e i v e
10. c o n c e i t e d

Spelling

11. ______________
12. ______________
13. ______________
14. ______________
15. ______________

Vocabulary

16. ______________
17. ______________
18. ______________
19. ______________

Alphabetizing

20. pool ______________ post

Reading Comprehension

(Worksheet 84, continued)

Motto of the United States

Do you know what a motto is? It is a saying that stands for what is important to a state, nation, family, or group. An early motto of the United States is **"E Pluribus Unum."** That is Latin for "Out of many, one." This motto appears on all U.S. coins. It is engraved on the dome of the U.S. **Capitol** Building in Washington, D.C. It is also part of our nation's shield, which appears on the back of the dollar bill. Benjamin Franklin, one of the chief leaders in our country's fight for independence, suggested the motto. It was decided in June of 1782 that this should be our nation's motto. As this country moves into the twenty-first **century,** the motto still has the same meaning. This country is a Great Melting Pot. It is made up of many people from many places. Yet, from the many, we are one country. "Out of many, one" is what this country stands for.

21. What does "E Pluribus Unum" mean? ______________________________

____

____

22. Who suggested "E Pluribus Unum" as our nation's motto? ______________

____

____

23. What is a motto?

- ○ Something that Benjamin Franklin made up
- ○ A saying that stands for something important
- ○ Part of our nation's shield
- ○ None of the above

24. When was it decided that "E Pluribus Unum" should be our nation's motto?

- ○ 1872
- ○ 1782
- ○ The 21st century
- ○ None of the above

25. How are the sayings "E Pluribus Unum" and "The Great Melting Pot" alike?

- ○ They were both suggested by Benjamin Franklin.
- ○ They mean that our nation is made up of many people joined together as one.
- ○ They appear on all U.S. coins.
- ○ None of the above

E Pluribus Unum: ē plur′ ə bəs yū′ nəm	**Capitol:** kăp′ ə təl	**century:** sĕnch′ ə rē

Name ______________________________

Teacher's Initials ______

Worksheet 85
Phonics Intervention
Sight Words, 12

Sight Word Review	**New Sight Words**
1. ______________	**11.** pour
2. ______________	**12.** Wednesday
3. ______________	**13.** course
4. ______________	**14.** Mr.
5. ______________	**15.** aunt
6. ______________	**16.** touch
7. ______________	**17.** Ms.
8. ______________	**18.** daughter
9. ______________	**19.** pull
10. ______________	**20.** hour

Sentence Completion

(Worksheet 85, continued)

aunt course daughter hour Mr.
Ms. pour pull touch Wednesday

21. The directions said to ____________ the cup of milk into the muffin mix and stir until moist.

22. My baby sister takes a daily nap that normally lasts about an ____________.

23. The barb on the end of the thorn made it extremely difficult to ____________ out of my finger.

24. I **love** (lŭv) my mother's sister, whom we call ____________ Jessie.

25. Of ____________! I would love to come to your birthday party. I'm surprised that you would feel that you had to ask.

26. My ________________ cannot understand why I want her to keep her room neat and clean.

27. My teacher, ____________ Greely, wore a cute denim skirt with a patchwork bear on it.

28. The weekday that falls right in the middle of the school week is ____________________.

29. "If you _____________ that wet oil paint, your fingertips will turn purple," warned my art instructor.

30. My twelve-year-old brother felt much older when the doctor called him ____________ Stanfield.

Name ______________________________

Teacher's Initials ______

Worksheet 86
Phonics Intervention
-ful, -ness

Coding and Reading

1. playful
2. basketful
3. cheerful
4. grateful
5. joyful
6. blackness
7. goodness
8. thickness
9. soreness
10. darkness

Spelling

11. ______________
12. ______________
13. ______________
14. ______________
15. ______________

Vocabulary

16. ______________
17. ______________
18. ______________
19. ______________
20. ______________
21. ______________

Alphabetizing

22. stripe struck strong stretch strap

____

____

____

____

____

Reading Comprehension

(Worksheet 86, continued)

The Boston Tea Party

Boston is the capital city of the state of **Massachusetts.** It was founded in 1630 by colonists from England. By 1750, Boston was an important seaport and center of trade. Many of the most thoughtful leaders of the independence movement came from Boston. The Boston Tea Party, one of the first acts of **rebellion** against England, took place in Boston. People in Boston were angry because England had placed a high tax on tea. They refused to buy tea from England. In November 1773, a ship from England holding 342 chests of tea landed in Boston Harbor. The citizens of Boston would not allow the tea to be unloaded, but England would not take back the tea until the tax was paid. In the darkness of night on December 16, some Boston citizens boarded the boat and dumped the tea into the harbor. This act showed that the American colonists were not **afraid** of the powerful forces of England. It was one more step that led to war against England. The first shot in that war was fired on **April** 19, 1775, on a bridge in a town not far from Boston. This shot is known as "the shot heard round the world."

23. When was Boston founded? ______________________________

____

24. Boston is the capital city of what state? ______________________________

____

25. Why did the people of Boston refuse to buy tea from England?

- ○ It was wet from being dumped in the harbor.
- ○ They did not want to pay the high tax England had put on tea.
- ○ They did not want to have to take it off the ship.
- ○ None of the above

26. When was the first shot of the war for independence fired?

- ○ November 1773
- ○ December 1773
- ○ April 1775
- ○ None of the above

27. Where was "the shot heard round the world" fired?

- ○ In Boston Harbor
- ○ In the center of Boston
- ○ In a town not far from Boston
- ○ None of the above

Massachusetts: mă sə chū´ səts **rebellion:** rĭ bĕl´ yən **afraid:** ə frād´
April: ā´ prəl

Name ______________________________

Teacher's Initials ______

Worksheet 87
Phonics Intervention

v|v

Coding and Reading

Circle the word that is coded correctly.

1. q u ī e t q u i ē t q u ī́ | ē t (ə)

2. c r ē a t e c r ĕ a t e c r ē | ā t e´

3. n ō e l n ṓ | ē l (ə) n ō | ĕ ĺ

4. m ḗ | o w m ē | o w´ m ē | ō w´

5. r ē a c t r ḗ | ă c t r ē | ă c t´

Trial by Jury

One of the most important rights granted in the Bill of Rights is a person's right to a speedy trial by a jury of his or her peers. The idea is that people just like you get to decide whether someone is **guilty** or innocent. It also means that a person accused of a crime cannot be jailed for a long time before he or she goes to trial. The person must be **proven** guilty. This means that a person is considered innocent until proven guilty. The jury is a group of **ordinary** citizens who listen to all of the evidence and decide whether the person accused of a crime is proven to have done the crime or not. A jury is created from a list of voters, taxpayers, and even people listed in the phone book. When citizens are sent letters asking them to be on jury duty, they must appear at the **courthouse.** They will be questioned by lawyers and by a judge, who will then decide which people can be fair enough to serve on the jury. Twelve people are picked to make up the jury. All twelve must **agree** before a person can be found guilty. Serving on a jury is a great duty. One day you might be asked to serve. Can you be fair?

6. How many people serve on a jury? ______________________________

____

____

7. What must be proven, a person's guilt or innocence? ______________________

____

____

8. Who makes up a jury of peers?

○ Ordinary people ○ Lawyers

○ Judges ○ None of the above

9. How does a jury decide whether a person is innocent or guilty?

○ They ask the judge to tell them. ○ Six of them tell the rest how to vote.

○ They ask the lawyers to tell them. ○ None of the above

10. What do you think is the most important thing a person on a jury must be?

○ A voter ○ A taxpayer

○ A fair person ○ None of the above

guilty: gĭl′ tē **proven:** prū′ vən **ordinary:** or′ dən ĕr ē
courthouse: kort′ hows **agree:** ə grē′

Name ______________________________

Teacher's Initials ______

Worksheet 88
Phonics Intervention
over-, pre-, under-

Coding and Reading

1. preheating
2. preschool
3. underexpose
4. underwater
5. overeating
6. overtime
7. prior
8. baldness
9. mystic
10. fearful

Spelling

11. ____________
12. ____________
13. ____________
14. ____________
15. ____________

Vocabulary

16. ____________
17. ____________
18. ____________
19. ____________
20. ____________
21. ____________

Alphabetizing

22. knock king key knot knight

____

____

____

____

____

Reading Comprehension

(Worksheet 88, continued)

The Statue of Liberty

On a small island overlooking New York Harbor stands a statue of a woman holding a torch overhead. This is the Statue of Liberty. The people of France gave this statue to the people of the United States over 100 years ago as a symbol of friendship. To many people the statue is also a symbol of hope and freedom. It was created in France by the sculptor **Auguste Bartholdi.** It was shipped to this country in the early 1880s. The statue is about 150 feet high with copper on the outside and **iron** underneath. A small island in New York Harbor was picked as the home for the statue. The only problem was that there was no base for the statue to be placed on. People from all parts of the United States donated money to build a base. At last, in October 1886, the statue was complete. A **celebration,** complete with fireworks, was held in New York Harbor. Today, people from all over the world visit the statue. They can go inside and walk up the 354 steps to its crown. There they can gaze out at New York Harbor and think about the meaning of liberty.

23. Which country gave the Statue of Liberty to the United States? ______________________

____

____

24. Who **designed** the Statue of Liberty? ______________________________

____

____

25. Why was the Statue of Liberty given as a gift?

- ○ As a token of peace
- ○ As a symbol of friendship
- ○ To celebrate the building of a base
- ○ None of the above

26. Who paid for the base of the Statue?

- ○ People from France
- ○ People from New York City
- ○ People from all over this country
- ○ None of the above

27. What does the Statue of Liberty mean to many people today?

- ○ It is a symbol of hope and freedom.
- ○ It is a symbol of France.
- ○ It is a symbol of hard work.
- ○ None of the above

Auguste Bartholdi: ō gūst′ bar tŏl′ dē **iron:** ī′ ern
celebration: sĕl ə brā′ shən **designed:** dĭ zīnd′

Name ______________________________

Teacher's Initials ______

Worksheet 89
Phonics Intervention
-es

Coding and Reading

1. b e a c h e s

2. s l y n e s s

3. m a r c h e s

4. w a t c h f u l

5. b r u s h e s

6. u n d e r r a t e

7. s u f f i x e s

8. o v e r m i x e s

9. f l u i d

10. p r e m i x e s

Spelling

11. ______________

12. ______________

13. ______________

14. ______________

15. ______________

Vocabulary

16. ______________

17. ______________

18. ______________

19. ______________

20. ______________

21. ______________

Alphabetizing

22. travel trap truffle tend term

____

____

____

____

____

Reading Comprehension

(Worksheet 89, continued)

Basketball

A player dribbles a ball down the **court.** The player stops, jumps, and shoots. The ball swishes through a net, and the crowd goes wild. You probably know this game as basketball, but did you know that it was invented in this country? In 1891, a man named James **Naismith** wanted to find a sport that could be played indoors on cold days. With a soccer ball and two peach baskets, Naismith created the game of basketball. He hung the baskets on the walls of a gym and players passed the ball until one team was able to throw it into its basket. Then the game stopped because the players had to take the ball out of the peach basket and start again. The game caught on quickly. By the late 1890s, there was a men's basketball **league.** Games were played in large arenas, and people paid to watch them. There have been many changes since the days of James Naismith. For one thing, there is a hole in the bottom of the basket now so players don't have to stop the game to get the ball back. The men's league is now the NBA. In 1996, women started their own league, the WNBA. We have come a long way from soccer balls and peach baskets!

23. Who invented basketball? ____________________

____

____

24. When was basketball invented? ____________________

____

____

25. Why was basketball invented?
- ○ To find a use for peach baskets
- ○ To think of new ways to use soccer balls
- ○ To find a sport that could be played indoors on cold days
- ○ None of the above

26. What did Naismith use as baskets?
- ○ Metal hoops
- ○ Old boxes
- ○ Peach baskets
- ○ None of the above

27. When did women form their own basketball league?
- ○ In 1891
- ○ In 1899
- ○ In 1996
- ○ None of the above

court: kort	**Naismith:** nā′ smĭth	**league:** lēg

Name ______________________________

Teacher's Initials ______

Worksheet 90
Phonics Intervention
Spelling with Final *c*

Spelling Bingo

ce	tch	ay	ge
k	dge	ve	ke
ss	a	s	ck
c	j	ee	es

Spelling

1. ______________
2. ______________
3. ______________
4. ______________
5. ______________

Vocabulary

6. ______________
7. ______________
8. ______________
9. ______________
10. ______________
11. ______________

Name ______________________________

Teacher's Initials ______

Worksheet 91

Phonics Intervention

Review of Sight Words

Sight Word Review

1. ______________
2. ______________
3. ______________
4. ______________
5. ______________
6. ______________
7. ______________
8. ______________
9. ______________
10. ______________

Spelling

11. ______________
12. ______________
13. ______________
14. ______________
15. ______________

Vocabulary

16. ______________
17. ______________
18. ______________
19. ______________
20. ______________
21. ______________

Alphabetizing

22. input
inner • insert

____

Complete Sight Word List

(Worksheet 91, continued)

- ☐ above
- ☐ again
- ☐ against
- ☐ answer
- ☐ any
- ☐ are
- ☐ aunt
- ☐ beautiful
- ☐ because
- ☐ been
- ☐ bought
- ☐ brother
- ☐ brought
- ☐ build
- ☐ busy
- ☐ buy
- ☐ caught
- ☐ certain
- ☐ climb
- ☐ clothes
- ☐ come
- ☐ cough
- ☐ could
- ☐ country
- ☐ course
- ☐ cousin
- ☐ daughter
- ☐ didn't
- ☐ do
- ☐ does
- ☐ done
- ☐ don't
- ☐ door
- ☐ Dr.
- ☐ enough
- ☐ early
- ☐ earth
- ☐ eye
- ☐ father
- ☐ February
- ☐ floor
- ☐ fought
- ☐ four
- ☐ friend
- ☐ from
- ☐ full
- ☐ give
- ☐ gone
- ☐ guard
- ☐ guess
- ☐ guest
- ☐ half
- ☐ have
- ☐ heard
- ☐ heart
- ☐ hour
- ☐ island
- ☐ laugh
- ☐ learn
- ☐ listen
- ☐ live
- ☐ many
- ☐ mother
- ☐ mountain
- ☐ move
- ☐ Mr.
- ☐ Mrs.
- ☐ Ms.
- ☐ none
- ☐ nothing
- ☐ ocean
- ☐ of
- ☐ often
- ☐ once
- ☐ one
- ☐ only
- ☐ other
- ☐ poor
- ☐ pour
- ☐ prove
- ☐ pull
- ☐ push
- ☐ put
- ☐ rough
- ☐ said
- ☐ says
- ☐ shoe
- ☐ should
- ☐ shoulder
- ☐ sign
- ☐ special
- ☐ some
- ☐ stomach
- ☐ straight
- ☐ sugar
- ☐ sure
- ☐ talk
- ☐ tastes
- ☐ taught
- ☐ their
- ☐ there
- ☐ they
- ☐ though
- ☐ thought
- ☐ through
- ☐ to
- ☐ touch
- ☐ tough
- ☐ trouble
- ☐ two
- ☐ very
- ☐ walk
- ☐ want
- ☐ was
- ☐ Wednesday
- ☐ were
- ☐ what
- ☐ where
- ☐ who
- ☐ whose
- ☐ woman
- ☐ women
- ☐ would
- ☐ young

Name ______________________________

Teacher's Initials ______

Worksheet 92

Phonics Intervention

´[sion, ´[ture

Coding and Reading

1. nurture
2. conclusion
3. vulture
4. permission
5. scripture
6. version
7. creature
8. explosion
9. moisture
10. succession

Spelling

11. ______________
12. ______________
13. ______________
14. ______________
15. ______________

Vocabulary

16. ______________
17. ______________
18. ______________
19. ______________
20. ______________
21. ______________

Alphabetizing

22. expression
expert • express

____

Reading Comprehension

(Worksheet 92, continued)

The City of San Francisco

Located on the coast of **California,** San Francisco is a center for industry, education, and culture. Founded as a military post in 1776, it was a small town for many years. Then in 1848, gold was found in the nearby hills. In the next 12 years, this small town had an explosion in its population and quickly grew into a large city of over 50,000 people! In 1906, an earthquake **destroyed** the city, but it was quickly built up again. Today, San Francisco is a place where many people like to live, to work, and to visit. San Francisco has a modern high-speed transit system known as BART, which stands for "Bay **Area** Rapid Transit," but visitors like to ride the famous cable cars to the tops of San Francisco's many hills. From there they can see San Francisco Bay, one of the world's most beautiful harbors; this always leaves a lasting impression. They can also take pictures of the **Golden** Gate Bridge, a structure that is a symbol of the city. Another symbol of the city is its willingness to adapt to new ideas. For example, San Francisco had one of the first women mayors, **Dianne Feinstein,** who was elected in 1978. She served until 1992, when she was elected to the U.S. **Senate.**

23. Where is San Francisco located? ______________________________

____

____

24. When was San Francisco founded? ______________________________

____

____

25. What caused people to begin to move to San Francisco after 1848?

- ○ The rapid transit system
- ○ The city's famous cable cars
- ○ Gold was found in nearby hills.
- ○ None of the above

26. What structure is a symbol of San Francisco?

- ○ The Golden Gate Bridge
- ○ San Francisco Bay
- ○ BART
- ○ None of the above

27. In 1978, Dianne Feinstein was elected to what position?

- ○ U.S. Senate
- ○ Mayor of San Francisco
- ○ Head of BART
- ○ None of the above

California: kă lə for′ nyə **destroyed:** dĭ stroid′ **Area:** ăr′ ē ə
Golden: gōl′ dən **Dianne Feinstein:** dī ăn′ fīn′ stīn **Senate:** sĕn′ ət

Name ______________________________

Teacher's Initials ______

Worksheet 93
Phonics Intervention
dis-, im-, in-, ir-, un-

Coding and Reading

1. unexpected
2. unwise
3. improper
4. indecent
5. disinfect
6. disconnect
7. irregular
8. fracture
9. confusion
10. admission

Spelling

11. ____________
12. ____________
13. ____________
14. ____________
15. ____________

Vocabulary

16. ____________
17. ____________
18. ____________
19. ____________
20. ____________
21. ____________

Alphabetizing

22. mimic

midway • milk

____

Reading Comprehension

The United States Congress

Members of Congress are elected by the people to make laws for the country. Congress is made up of two groups, the Senate and the House of **Representatives.** They meet in the Capitol building in Washington, D.C. There are 100 senators, two for each state. Members of the House are chosen according to the population of each state. Today, the House has 435 members. One of the most important jobs of Congress is to make laws. First, a representative or senator will introduce a bill, or an idea for a law. Then the bill is sent to a committee. Committee members discuss the bill's good and bad points. Sometimes they **disagree** with each other about the bill or are uncertain about the effect it will have on the country. They may even think of ways to improve the bill. If the committee **approves** the bill, it is sent back to the House or Senate. All the members then vote on whether or not the bill should become law. A **majority** of both the House and the Senate must **agree** on a bill before it can be passed. Then the bill is sent to the White House for the president to sign. When the president signs a bill, it becomes law.

23. What is the job of Congress? ______________________________

____

____

24. Where does Congress meet? ______________________________

____

____

25. How many senators are there?

- ○ 50
- ○ 100
- ○ 435
- ○ None of the above

26. Where is a bill sent once it is introduced?

- ○ To the president to be signed
- ○ To the Senate to be voted on
- ○ To a committee to be discussed
- ○ None of the above

27. Who has to sign a bill into law?

- ○ The House of Representatives
- ○ The president
- ○ The Senate
- ○ None of the above

Representatives: rĕp rĭ zĕnt′ ət ĭvz **disagree:** dĭs ə grē′
approves: ə prūvz′ **majority:** mə jor′ ə tē **agree:** ə grē′

Name ________________________________

Teacher's Initials ______

Worksheet 94
Phonics Intervention
´[cious, ´[tious

Coding and Reading

1. spacious
2. vicious
3. cautious
4. infectious
5. disinterested
6. mission
7. preconceive
8. vision
9. inspection
10. adventure

Spelling

11. ______________
12. ______________
13. ______________
14. ______________
15. ______________

Vocabulary

16. ______________
17. ______________
18. ______________
19. ______________
20. ______________
21. ______________

Alphabetizing

22. cent
census • certify

____

The Great **Mississippi**

More than 2,300 miles long, the Mississippi River is the longest river in the United States. The river, whose name means "Father of Waters" in the **Algonquin Indian language,** has long been used for travel and for shipping goods. If you look at a map of the United States, you will see that the river follows an irregular course. It seems to cut the United States in half from the north to the south. At one time the Mississippi River formed the western boundary of the United States. But in 1803, the United States bought the land west of the Mississippi from France. Since the Mississippi connects to many other rivers, it became a pathway for ambitious settlers pushing west in the early 1800s. In 1812, steamboats with their big paddle wheels were introduced. The big steamboats were fast and **reliable.** People could have their own rooms on the boats. They could eat delicious food. They could travel in comfort. Because of this, more and more people traveled on the river. Today the river is still used to ship goods. Now the steamboats carry people on the river for fun and to give people a chance to see what it was like to live on the great Mississippi.

23. How long is the Mississippi River? ______________________

____

____

24. What does the name "Mississippi" mean? ______________________

____

____

25. What are the main uses of the Mississippi River today?

- ○ Fishing
- ○ Swimming
- ○ Travel and shipping goods
- ○ None of the above

26. Why do you think people liked traveling on steamboats?

- ○ Steamboats were fast and reliable.
- ○ Steamboats had big paddle wheels.
- ○ Delicious food was served on steamboats.
- ○ All of the above

27. How does the course of the Mississippi look on a map?

- ○ Straight
- ○ Irregular
- ○ Short
- ○ None of the above

Mississippi: mĭ sə sĭp′ ē **reliable:** rĭ lī′ ə bəl
Algonquin Indian language: ăl gŏn′ kwən ĭn′ dē ən lăn′ gwĭj

Name ______________________________

Teacher's Initials ______

Worksheet 95
Phonics Intervention
-en, -ish, -ist, -ous

Coding and Reading

1. poisonous
2. thunderous
3. unselfish
4. sheepish
5. cartoonist
6. tourist
7. lighten
8. weaken
9. gracious
10. concession

Spelling

11. ______________
12. ______________
13. ______________
14. ______________
15. ______________

Vocabulary

16. ______________
17. ______________
18. ______________
19. ______________
20. ______________
21. ______________

Alphabetizing

22. well

weave • weep

____

Reading Comprehension

Memorial Day

The band leader raises a baton with a **flourish.** It is the signal for the start of the Memorial Day parade. Marchers move down the street. They include people in uniforms from all branches of the Armed Forces. At the parade's finish, the marchers encircle a monument to place a wreath **honoring** those who gave their lives serving their country in war. Memorial Day is a national holiday **celebrated** on the last Monday in May. It is a day for people to honor the memory of those who gave their lives for freedom. The first Memorial Day was on May 30, 1868. On that day, people remembered the Civil War dead. The Civil War was fought **between** 1861 and 1865. North fought against South over the right to enslave black people. The North won, slavery was abolished, and the country was united again. Remembering the dead on both sides was a symbol of the country coming together again. When we honor our war dead, it reminds us that no matter our differences, we all believe in freedom and in our glorious country.

23. When was Memorial Day first celebrated? ______________________________

____

____

24. When is Memorial Day celebrated now? ______________________________

____

____

25. Why do people celebrate Memorial Day?

- ○ To honor the American flag
- ○ To honor America
- ○ To honor those who gave their lives serving their country in war
- ○ None of the above

26. How is Memorial Day celebrated?

- ○ With a fireworks display
- ○ With a parade
- ○ With presents
- ○ None of the above

27. Who was honored on the first Memorial Day?

- ○ The dead of the Civil War
- ○ American citizens
- ○ People in government
- ○ None of the above

Memorial: mə mor′ ē əl **flourish:** flər′ ĭsh **honoring:** ŏn′ er ĭng
celebrated: sĕl′ ə brāt ĕd **between:** bĭ twēn′

Name ______________________________

Teacher's Initials ______

Doubling/Dropping Rules

To begin, make:

1 check mark if the root word ends with **one** vowel and **one** consonant *and* the final syllable is **accented.**

1 check mark if the root word ends with a **silent *e*.**

1 check mark if the suffix is a **vowel suffix.**

When finished:

If you have **2** check marks, **double the final consonant** or **drop the silent *e*** before adding the suffix.

If you have **fewer than 2** check marks, just **add the suffix.**

	☐		☐		
1.	open	+	ed	=	______________
2.	repel	+	ing	=	______________
3.	enter	+	ed	=	______________
4.	resort	+	ing	=	______________
5.	result	+	ed	=	______________
6.	admit	+	ed	=	______________

Vocabulary

7. ____________________

8. ____________________

9. ____________________

10. ____________________

11. ____________________

12. ____________________

Alphabetizing

13. binge
birth • black

____

Name ______________________________

Teacher's Initials ______

Worksheet 97
Phonics Intervention
v´|ccv, v|ccv´

Coding and Reading

1. afloat
2. respect
3. supreme
4. migrate
5. deflate
6. hydrant
7. between
8. brochure
9. zebra
10. across

Spelling

11. ______________
12. ______________
13. ______________
14. ______________
15. ______________

Vocabulary

16. ______________
17. ______________
18. ______________
19. ______________
20. ______________
21. ______________

Alphabetizing

22. perfection

______________ • ______________

Reading Comprehension

Members of Congress

Members of the U.S. Congress belong to the Senate or the House of Representatives. Each state has two senators, but different numbers of representatives. The 435 House members are elected by the people who live in a district in their home state. A district has a population of about 500,000. States with big populations have more representatives in the House than states with small populations. Senators run for **reelection** every six years. Members of the House are elected every two years.

At one time, all members of Congress were white men. As the nation has changed, so has the makeup of Congress. In 1916, **Jeanette Rankin** of Montana was the first woman elected to the House of Representatives. **Margaret Chase Smith** of Maine was the first woman elected to both the House and the Senate. In 1966, **Edward Brooke** of Massachusetts was the first black man elected to the Senate, and in 1968, **Shirley Chisholm** of New York was the first black woman elected to the House of Representatives. In 1992, Dianne Feinstein of California was elected to the Senate with the largest majority ever recorded for a senator. Respect your congresspeople. They work for you!

23. How many representatives are there in the House of Representatives? ____________

____

24. How many senators are there from each state? ____________________

____

25. How often does a representative run for office?

- ○ Every four years
- ○ Every two years
- ○ Every six years
- ○ None of the above

26. How do people become members of the House of Representatives?

- ○ They are appointed by the president.
- ○ They are appointed by the Speaker of the House.
- ○ They are elected by the people of their district.
- ○ None of the above

27. Who was the first woman elected to the Senate?

- ○ Shirley Chisholm
- ○ Jeanette Rankin
- ○ Dianne Feinstein
- ○ None of the above

reelection: rē ə lĕk′ shən **Jeanette Rankin:** jə nĕt′ răn′ kən
Margaret Chase Smith: mar′ grət chās smĭth
Edward Brooke: ĕd′ werd brŏŏk **Shirley Chisholm:** sher′ lē chĭz′ əm

Name ______________________________

Teacher's Initials ______

Worksheet 98

Phonics Intervention

iç¢, il¢, in¢

Coding and Reading

1. mobile
2. crevice
3. famine
4. engine
5. fragile
6. jaundice
7. machine
8. magazine
9. automobile
10. routine

Spelling

11. ________________
12. ________________
13. ________________
14. ________________
15. ________________

Vocabulary

16. ________________
17. ________________
18. ________________
19. ________________
20. ________________
21. ________________

Alphabetizing

22. elementary

________________ • ________________

Reading Comprehension

(Worksheet 98, continued)

The Great Seal of the United States

The Great Seal of the United States appears on **treaties** with other nations, on letters signed by the president, and on the back of the $1 bill, among other places. At the center of the Great Seal is an American bald eagle. On the eagle's chest is a shield with 13 red and white stripes, which stand for the 13 colonies. In its right talon, or claw, is an **olive** branch, a symbol of peace. In its left talon the eagle holds 13 arrows, a symbol of might. Entwined in its beak is a banner with our national motto: E Pluribus Unum. Overhead are 13 stars, which stand for the first 13 states.

The planning of the Great Seal began in the early 1780s. Many people had ideas for the Great Seal. For example, Benjamin Franklin suggested the American wild turkey as one possible symbol. People in Congress compiled and **reviewed** all the ideas. They chose the bald eagle rather than a wild turkey because they felt it was a more powerful symbol. The Great Seal was designed by **William** Barton. Using a special cutting device, he engraved the seal on a metal plate. The Great Seal was approved by the U.S. Congress in 1789. The seal reminds the world that we are a peaceful nation, but one that is powerful enough to defend our freedom and way of life.

23. What is at the center of the Great Seal? ______________________________

____

____

24. What symbol on the seal stands for peace? ______________________________

____

____

25. What is the symbol of the 13 arrows on the seal?

- ○ A symbol of peace
- ○ A symbol of power and might
- ○ The first 13 states
- ○ None of the above

26. Who designed the Great Seal?

- ○ Benjamin Franklin
- ○ Congress
- ○ William Barton
- ○ None of the above

27. Where does the Great Seal appear?

- ○ On the U.S. flag
- ○ On the $5 bill
- ○ On the front of a penny
- ○ None of the above

treaties: trē′ tēz	**olive:** ŏ′ lĭv	**reviewed:** rē vyūd′	**William:** wĭl′ yəm

Name ______________________________

Teacher's Initials ______

Worksheet 99

Phonics Intervention

mono-, bi-, tri-, quad-, pent-, eigh

Coding and Reading

1. b i c e p s
2. t r i c e p s
3. g l a m o r o u s
4. m o n o p l a n e
5. g o p h e r
6. t r i g r a p h
7. m a r i n e
8. g e s t u r e
9. w e i g h t
10. s l e i g h

Spelling

11. ______________
12. ______________
13. ______________
14. ______________
15. ______________

Vocabulary

16. ______________
17. ______________
18. ______________
19. ______________
20. ______________
21. ______________

Alphabetizing

22. trumpet

______________ • ______________

Reading Comprehension

The City of Washington, D.C.

Washington, D.C., is our nation's capital. It is the home of the president of the United States and the U.S. Congress. Not far from Washington is the Pentagon, the headquarters of our Armed Forces. The city was designed by **Pierre L'Enfant** in 1791. He divided the city into four quadrants with the U.S. Capitol at the center. A long mall leads from the Capitol to the **Potomac** River. This is the Mall where people gathered in 1963 to hear Martin Luther King, Jr. speak of his dream for equal rights. Along the Mall are museums, monuments, and memorials such as the one to veterans of the **Vietnam** War. There is much to see and do in Washington, D.C. You can visit the Federal Triangle with its many beautiful government buildings. In the National **Archives** Building, the original **copies** of the Declaration of Independence, the Constitution, and the Bill of Rights are displayed. Although Washington, D.C., is a busy city, it is easy to find a quiet spot. Many people run or bicycle along the paths in Rock Creek Park. Others take walking tours to visit the beautiful homes and shops of one of Washington's most famous neighborhoods, Georgetown. Washington, D.C., is a city of great **beauty** and a place of great history.

23. Who designed Washington, D.C.? ______________________________

____

24. What building stands at the center of Washington, D.C.? ____________________

____

25. How was Washington, D.C., designed to be divided?

- ○ Into eight parts
- ○ Into four quadrants
- ○ Into six parts
- ○ None of the above

26. What famous event took place on the Mall?

- ○ Congress met.
- ○ The Bill of Rights was displayed.
- ○ Martin Luther King, Jr. spoke of his dream for equal rights.
- ○ None of the above

27. Where can you see the original copy of the Constitution?

- ○ In the Capitol Building
- ○ In the National Archives Building
- ○ In the White House
- ○ None of the above

Pierre L'Enfant: pē ăr′ lŏn fŏn′ **Potomac:** pə tō′ mək **Vietnam:** vē ĕt nŏm′
Archives: ar′ kīvz **copies:** kŏ′ pēz **beauty:** byū′ tē

Name ______________________________

Teacher's Initials ______

Changing Rule

If the root word ends with vowel *y*, change *y* to *i* before adding a suffix (except for suffixes beginning with *i*).

Do not change *y* if it comes after a vowel because it is part of a digraph or a diphthong.

1. plenty + ful = ______________
2. mercy + less = ______________
3. tally + ing = ______________
4. bulky + ness = ______________
5. bounty + ful = ______________
6. flimsy + er = ______________
7. handy + ness = ______________
8. try + ing = ______________
9. sleepy + er = ______________
10. happy + ness = ______________

Vocabulary

11. ____________________

12. ____________________

13. ____________________

14. ____________________

15. ____________________

16. ____________________

Alphabetizing

17. happiest

________________ • ________________

Vowel Rules

Vowel Rule 1: A vowel followed by a consonant is short; code it with a breve. *(Lesson 2)*

v̆c

căt lŏg sĭt tŭg wĕt

Vowel Rule 2: An open, accented vowel is long; code it with a macron. *(Lesson 3)*

v̄´→

ā´ flū´ hī´ mē´ sō´

Vowel Rule 3: A vowel followed by a consonant and a silent *e* is long; code the vowel with a macron and cross out the sneaky *e*. *(Lesson 17)*

v̄–e̸

hōpe̸ līke̸ nāme̸ rūle̸ thēse̸

Vowel Rule 4: An open, unaccented *a* is usually schwa; the letters *e*, *o*, and *u* are usually long; and the letter *i* is usually short. *(Lesson 78)*

å b å | n ă n´ | å

v→ ē ō ū ē | r ā s e̸´ h ō | t ĕ l´ J ū | l ȳ´

ĭ d ĭ | v ī d e̸´

PHONICS RULES

Spelling Rules

/ch/

Final /ch/ Rules *(Lesson 72)*

tch after a **short vowel**

crutch etch match notch stitch

ch after **anything else**

bench ouch pooch porch

/f/, /l/, or /s/

Floss Rule: When a one-syllable root word has a **short vowel** sound followed by the sound /f/, /l/, or /s/, it is usually spelled ff, ll, or ss. *(Lesson 44)*

ff	ll	ss
cuff	doll	boss
puff	hill	miss
sniff	well	pass

/j/

Initial and Medial /j/ Rules *(Lesson 64)*

j before **a, o,** or **u**

jam joke jug

g before **e, i,** or **y**

German giant stingy

Final /j/ Rules *(Lesson 71)*

dge after a **short vowel**

badge bridge edge judge lodge

ge after **anything else**

cage charge lunge stooge

PHONICS RULES

/k/

Initial and Medial /k/ Rules *(Lesson 12)*

k before **e, i,** or **y**

keg kid milky

c before **a, o, u,** or any **consonant**

cat cot cup pact

Final /k/ Rules *(Lesson 13)*

ck after a **short vowel** *(Lesson 13)*

black duck lock neck sick

k after a **consonant** or a **vowel digraph** *(Lesson 38)*

bank book milk week

ke after a **long vowel** *(Lesson 50)*

broke duke like make

c at the end of a word with two or more **syllables** *(Lesson 90)*

Atlantic garlic magic picnic

/s/

Final /s/ Rules *(Lesson 54)*

ss after a **short vowel**

boss dress fuss grass miss

ce after a **long vowel**

ice space truce

se after **anything else**

crease false horse house loose

/v/

Final /v/ Rule: When a word has the final sound /v/, it is spelled **ve**. *(Lesson 50)*

have hive leave live solve wave

(Some of these words may be irregular for reading since they will appear to follow the vowel-consonant-e rule.)

Suffixes

Adding a Consonant Suffix: To spell a word with a consonant suffix, just add the suffix to the end of the root word. *(Lesson 27)*

cake + s = cakes care + ful = careful close + ly = closely

hat + less = hatless red + ness = redness

Adding a Vowel Suffix

Doubling Rule: When the final syllable of a word is accented and it ends with one vowel and one consonant, double the final consonant before adding a vowel suffix. *(Lesson 60)*

hit′ + ing = hitting omit′ + ing = omitting run′ + er = runner

Dropping Rule: When a word ends with a silent *e*, drop the **e** before adding a vowel suffix. *(Lesson 80)*

make + ing = making rule + er = ruler

Changing Rule: *(Lesson 100)*

If a root word ends with vowel **y,** change **y** to **i** before adding a suffix (except for suffixes beginning with *i*).

silly + ness = silliness

Do not change **y** if it comes after a vowel because it is part of a digraph or a diphthong.

play + ed = played

How to Divide and Label a Word

(Lesson 15)

v c | c v

n a p k i n
v   v

n a p k i n
v c c v

n a p | k i n
v c | c v

n a p´ | k i n
v c | c v

n ă p´ | k ĭ n
v c | c v

v c c v

1. v c´|c v — năp´|kĭn (v c|c v)
   (Lesson 15)

2. v c|c v´ — ĭn|jĕct´ (v c|c v)

3. v|c c v´ — rē|spĕct´ ing (v|c c v)
   (Lesson 97)

4. v´|c c v — cō´|brə (v|c c v)

(Lesson 59)

ĭm|pŏr´|tənt (v c|c v c|c v)

VCV

1. V́|CV

(Lesson 65)

bā́|bẏ
v|c v

2. VĆ|V

(Lesson 75)

rŏb́|ĭns
v c |v

3. V|CV́

(Lessons 77 and 78)

ē|rāsé
v|c v

hō|tĕĺ
v|c v

Jū|lȳ́
v|c v

bă|năń|ă
v|c v c |v

dĭ|vīdé
v|c v

vcccv

(Lesson 62)

1. v c|c c v — ĕ x|p l ā i n′ (v c|c c v)

2. v c c|c v — p ŭ m p′|k ĭ n (v c c|c v)

(The accent may appear on either syllable.)

vv

(Lesson 87)

1. v′|v — d ī′|ĕ t (v|v)

2. v|v′ — c r ē|ā t e′ (v|v)

3. v|v — c ă m′|ē|ō (v|v)

Syllable Division Procedure

1. **Code any affixes and final, stable syllables.**

2. **Code any "obvious coding."** ("Obvious coding" is any coding except for coding on *top* of vowels[†] or coding that cannot be determined until a word is pronounced, such as the coding for a voiced sound.)

   k-back *c*'s (usually found before *a*, *o*, *u*, or any consonant or at the end of multisyllabic words)
   cedilla *c*'s (usually found before *e*, *i*, or *y*)
   soft *g*'s (usually found before *e*, *i*, or *y*)
   silent *e*'s (usually found at the end of words)
   vowel *y*'s (dot only; usually found in medial or final position)
   digraphs, trigraphs, quadrigraphs (underline only)
   combinations
   diphthongs

3. **If the word contains more than two vowels, begin identifying the vowel pattern:**
   a. Label the vowels. (Do not label silent *e*'s or vowels in an affix or final, stable syllable.)
   b. Label the consonants between those vowels.
   c. Determine the syllable division pattern.
   d. Divide the word. (Refer to the syllable division rules to determine where a particular syllable division pattern may be divided.)
   e. Place the accent. (Refer to the syllable division rules to determine which syllable may be accented.)

4. **Code the remaining vowels.**

5. **Read the word.** If the word is not recognized, try any of the following before rereading:[††]
   a. Move the accent to a different syllable. (Refer to the syllable division rules for help.)
   b. Redivide the word. (Refer to the syllable division rules for help.)
   c. Try alternate sounds for letters/letter clusters that make multiple sounds:
      ar, ch, ea, ei, ie, oo, or, ou, ow, th, vowel *y*
   d. Try alternate vowel sounds. (e.g., A vowel may make a schwa sound in an unaccented syllable.)
   e. See if any two vowels that may have looked like diphthongs or digraphs are actually part of a "vv" syllable division pattern (e.g., "create"); if so, erase all coding and repeat the syllable division process.

Remember that there are exceptions to every rule listed above. Flexibility is essential when dividing and coding words.

PHONICS RULES

[†]Vowel *y* is an exception. Students should dot the *y* but postpone any additional coding until they read the word and determine which vowel sound it is making.

[††]These are listed in no particular order.

Letter Cluster Chart A

Consonant Digraphs

 ch		 ch		 çh	
 ck		ng		ph	
sh		th		th	

Vowel Digraphs

āi		ĕa		ew		ŏo	
au		eā	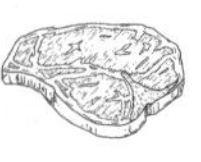	ēy		ōo	
aw		ēe		īe		oū	
āy	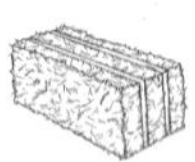	ēi		iē	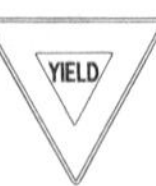	ōw	
ēa		ei		ōa		ūe	

Ghost Letter Digraphs

gn		 kn		wr	

PHONICS RUES

Letter Cluster Chart B

Trigraphs

igh  

dge 

tch  

Combinations

er 

ir  

qu  

ar´ 

or´ 

ur 

ar 

or  

wh 

ar 

or  

Diphthongs

oi 

ou 

ow 

oy 

Quadrigraph

eigh 

Final, Stable Syllables

[ble  

[sion 

[dle 

[sion 

[fle 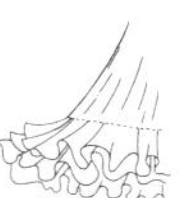

[tion 

[gle 

[ture 

[ple  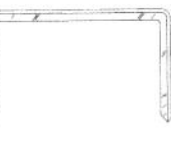

[cious 

[tle 

[tious 

Name ________________________________

Teacher's Initials ______

Assessment 1
Phonics Intervention
(Give anytime after Lesson 6)

Coding and Reading

1. b u g
2. b i t
3. w e t
4. n o t
5. h i s
6. g a l
7. m e t
8. a s
9. j o g
10. w e
11. t a g
12. c u t
13. m i t t
14. r o t
15. s o

Spelling

16. ____________________
17. ____________________
18. ____________________
19. ____________________
20. ____________________

Vocabulary

21. ____________________
22. ____________________
23. ____________________
24. ____________________
25. ____________________
26. ____________________

Alphabetizing

27. lad not sip

____

____

____

ASSESSMENTS

Name ______________________________

Teacher's Initials ______

Assessment 2
Phonics Intervention
(Give anytime after Lesson 12)

ASSESSMENTS

Coding and Reading

1. b e s t
2. m i s s
3. g o
4. p r i n t
5. h o p
6. f r o
7. s c a n
8. s t r a n d
9. h e
10. s w a m
11. s w i f t
12. t e l l
13. t r u s t
14. w i n
15. y a k

Spelling

16. ______________
17. ______________
18. ______________
19. ______________
20. ______________

Vocabulary

21. ______________
22. ______________
23. ______________
24. ______________
25. ______________
26. ______________

Alphabetizing

27. big fun can

____

____

____

Name ______________________________

Teacher's Initials ______

Assessment 3
Phonics Intervention
(Give anytime after Lesson 18)

Coding and Reading

1. c h i l l

2. t h r i l l

3. s h r i m p

4. s o

5. s p l i n t

6. s h e l f

7. t h u m p

8. t r y

9. s h e

10. t h i s

Spelling

11. ____________

12. ____________

13. ____________

14. ____________

15. ____________

Vocabulary

16. ____________

17. ____________

18. ____________

19. ____________

20. ____________

21. ____________

Alphabetizing

22. fad net bag

____

____

____

ASSESSMENTS

Mom will hum as she sets the plants by the pond. She will ban the dogs if the plants get dug up.

23. What will Mom set by the pond? ______________________

____

____

24. What will she ban? ______________________

____

____

Name ______________________________

Teacher's Initials ______

Assessment 4
Phonics Intervention
(Give anytime after Lesson 24)

Coding and Reading

1. grain
2. ray
3. deed
4. long
5. escape
6. cheap
7. roast
8. rescue
9. valley
10. stuck

Spelling

11. ______________
12. ______________
13. ______________
14. ______________
15. ______________

Vocabulary

16. ______________
17. ______________
18. ______________
19. ______________
20. ______________
21. ______________

Alphabetizing

22. melt must mash

____

____

____

ASSESSMENTS

A rescue team had to rescue three pups in the fog. The pups' feet were stuck in the mud near a pond. One man on the rescue team was strong and lifted them from the mud as he hung from a damp tree branch.

23. What did the rescue team save? ______________________________

____

____

24. What did the strong man hang from? ______________________________

____

____

ASSESSMENTS

Name ______________________________

Teacher's Initials ______

Assessment 5
Phonics Intervention
(Give anytime after Lesson 30)

ASSESSMENTS

Coding and Reading

1. s m a s h

2. c h u r n

3. s t a l e

4. w i n g

5. f i r m

6. s i s t e r

7. s t a c k

8. c r y

9. h e r

10. m a t h

Spelling

11. ______________

12. ______________

13. ______________

14. ______________

15. ______________

Vocabulary

16. ______________

17. ______________

18. ______________

19. ______________

20. ______________

21. ______________

Alphabetizing

22. cloth egg hire

box ______________

____

deer ______________

____

____

Reading Comprehension

(Assessment 5, continued)

My sister, Jane, is in the first grade and can read as well as I can. She has three albums, but I like one the best. It is a big, red album with lots of splendid jokes, gags, and tricks. Jane likes to take it to class and teach tricks to the girls who eat lunch with her. We share some of the jokes with Mom and Dad as we eat dinner.

23. Who is in the first grade? ______________________________

____

____

24. What does Jane teach the girls at lunch? ______________________________

____

____

Name ______________________________

Teacher's Initials ______

Assessment 6
Phonics Intervention
(Give anytime after Lesson 36)

Coding and Reading

1. s t u f f e d
2. m a s k i n g
3. h o m e l e s s
4. s h i p s
5. w h i s p e r
6. q u a k e
7. t u r n i p s
8. l a n d e d
9. s t a y e d
10. s t e e p

Spelling

11. ______________
12. ______________
13. ______________
14. ______________
15. ______________

Vocabulary

16. ______________
17. ______________
18. ______________
19. ______________
20. ______________
21. ______________

Alphabetizing

22. hum alp damp dim fog

____

____

____

____

____

Sentence Completion

stuffed masking homeless ships whisper
quake turnips landed stayed steep

23. Clay was _____________ after eating six turkey legs.

24. The **icy** (ī′ sē) hill was so _____________ the truck was spinning its wheels.

25. My mom makes me eat _____________ when my dad **grows** (grōz) them in his garden.

26. The stray dog basked in the sun by the tree stumps but _____________ near the meat scraps.

27. "Don't _____________ in church," said my strict dad.

Name ______________________________

Teacher's Initials ______

Assessment 7
Phonics Intervention
(Give anytime after Lesson 42)

Coding and Reading

1. quill
2. whim
3. curling
4. worth
5. quail
6. warp
7. carpet (or carpet)
8. cord
9. dollar
10. doctor

Spelling

11. ______________
12. ______________
13. ______________
14. ______________
15. ______________

Vocabulary

16. ______________
17. ______________
18. ______________
19. ______________
20. ______________
21. ______________

Alphabetizing

22. clasp
   - ○ crust • damp
   - ○ cold • contest
   - ○ cart • cold

ASSESSMENTS

The Reids **live** (lĭv) on a farm, and on that farm they keep Buster, the horse. Buster is a black-and-white paint horse. The Reids raise corn to sell and to feed Buster in the winter. When the Reids run short of corn for Buster, Sam Reid feeds him hay. Buster snorts when Sam does that and tries to get Sam to **give** (gĭv) him some corn. Sam thinks it is neat that Buster can tell him that he likes corn better than hay.

23. What do the Reids raise? ______________________

____

____

24. When does Buster get hay? ______________________

____

____

Name ______________________________

Teacher's Initials ______

Assessment 8
Phonics Intervention
(Give anytime after Lesson 48)

Coding and Reading

1. s l i c k e s t

2. k i n d

3. t r a c k e r

4. l o o k e d

5. s q u i n t

6. w h i t t l e

7. h a r p o o n

8. c o a c h

9. c l u e

10. s h e l t e r

Spelling

11. ______________

12. ______________

13. ______________

14. ______________

15. ______________

Vocabulary

16. ______________

17. ______________

18. ______________

19. ______________

20. ______________

21. ______________

Alphabetizing

22. mother ______________ ocean

ASSESSMENTS

Glenn was seeking a tool in the thick brush. A bee, hidden in the leaves, stung him on the neck. In his effort to escape the bee, Glenn slipped on a slick rock and landed on a cactus. Glenn felt sick and wished that he were home. As he stood up, he spotted the tool he was looking for. He picked up the tool and limped home to get first aid.

23. What was Glenn seeking? ______________________________

____

____

24. What made Glenn slip? ______________________________

____

____

Name ____________________

Teacher's Initials ______

Assessment 9

Phonics Intervention

(Give anytime after Lesson 54)

Coding and Reading

1. s p h e r e
2. m a r b l e
3. p u d d l e
4. d i m p l e
5. s c u f f l e
6. b u g l e s
7. c r a d l e
8. h a s s l e
9. c o r n e r
10. m a s h i n g

Spelling

11. ____________
12. ____________
13. ____________
14. ____________
15. ____________

Vocabulary

16. ____________
17. ____________
18. ____________
19. ____________
20. ____________
21. ____________

Alphabetizing

22. shirt she shy

____

____

____

ASSESSMENTS

It had been a hard day. Steph sailed in the bay and got too far from shore. A shark swam by the boat and startled her so that she let go of the sail. The wind whipped the sail, which then hit Steph on the nose. Her nose started to bleed, and Steph had to use her good shirt to stop the bleeding. It started to rain, so Steph grabbed the sail and started back to shore. She was so glad when she landed that she ran home in the rain and forgot to tie up her boat.

23. What startled Steph? ______________________________

____

____

24. What did Steph use for her bleeding nose? ______________________________

____

____

Name ______________________________

Teacher's Initials ______

Assessment 10
Phonics Intervention
(Give anytime after Lesson 60)

Coding and Reading

1. wreck

2. knot

3. gnat

4. candy

5. sty

6. leash

7. thread

8. steak

9. fussy

10. circus

Spelling

11. ______________

12. ______________

13. ______________

14. ______________

15. ______________

Vocabulary

16. ______________

17. ______________

18. ______________

19. ______________

20. ______________

21. ______________

Alphabetizing

22. cob collar coffee

coach______________

____

coddle______________

____

____

ASSESSMENTS

Reading Comprehension

Vince's hands were *clammy*, or damp, with fear, and the feeling was wrecking his lunch. He could not wait for the sun to set and the fear to *subside*, or lessen. Vince felt better knowing that his mom and dad would be with him. His little brother would be there too. The gnashing and clenching of his teeth did not help Vince forget his fear. He wrote plays on a pad so he would not forget them. When it was time, Vince headed to the car and his knees buckled. The first soccer game got to him each year!

23. What does "subside" mean? ______________________________

____

____

24. Why was Vince **full** (fŏŏl) of fear? ______________________________

____

____

Name ______________________________

Teacher's Initials ______

Assessment 11
Phonics Intervention
(Give anytime after Lesson 66)

Coding and Reading

1. soy

2. spoil

3. crowd

4. hollow

5. found

6. soup

7. center

8. chimpanzee

9. wrote

10. sparkle

Spelling

11. ______________

12. ______________

13. ______________

14. ______________

15. ______________

Vocabulary

16. ______________

17. ______________

18. ______________

19. ______________

20. ______________

21. ______________

Alphabetizing

22. teach them trace thick tar

____

____

____

____

____

ASSESSMENTS

Reading Comprehension

Phil, Steve, and Calvin have a rock band. One day, while playing at Steve's house in town, the boys had a guest. A **neighbor** (nā′ bər) came to the house and asked them to lower the sound, or he would have to turn them in for disturbing the peace. The boys did not want to **cause** (kŏz) any problems, so Phil offered to let them use his house. (His house, which was three miles from town, was far from other people's homes.) The boys started to play at Phil's house so the people who lived near Steve would not get upset.

23. Who is in the band? ______________________________

____

____

24. Why do the boys play at Phil's house now?

- ○ His house is bigger.
- ○ They don't want to disturb neighbors.
- ○ They like to drive three miles.

25. What is "disturbing the peace"?

- ○ Being too loud
- ○ Being in a band
- ○ Playing at Phil's house

Name ______________________________

Teacher's Initials ______

Assessment 12
Phonics Intervention
(Give anytime after Lesson 72)

Coding and Reading

1. margin
2. booklet
3. partly
4. trucker
5. loudest
6. charge
7. Wisconsin
8. lobster
9. spider
10. pillow

Spelling

11. ______________
12. ______________
13. ______________
14. ______________
15. ______________

Vocabulary

16. ______________
17. ______________
18. ______________
19. ______________
20. ______________
21. ______________

Alphabetizing

22. flimsy ______________ graph

At twelve-thirty, a girl in our school left to get a drink to quench her thirst. She drove to the nearest store, parked her car, and went inside to get her drink. While she was in the store, her car started rolling. The girl stumbled on a cable as she ran outside to catch her car. She fell to the ground but quickly got back up and ran down the road. Her car barely missed a puddle of oil, some loose wood in the street, and three bottles that had been thrown from a car. The girl jumped in her car and stepped on the brakes just as the car slowed from going up a hill. She was so happy that her car was intact.

23. What made the girl stumble? ______________________________

____

____

24. In the last sentence, what must the word "intact" mean?

- ○ Not wrecked
- ○ **Full** (fo͝ol) of gas
- ○ Not rolling

25. Why did the car slow down?

- ○ It ran out of gas.
- ○ A tire went flat.
- ○ It rolled up a hill.

Name ______________________________

Teacher's Initials ______

Assessment 13
Phonics Intervention
(Give anytime after Lesson 78)

Coding and Reading

1. might

2. stretcher

3. dodge

4. subdue

5. bench

6. over

7. chord

8. chef

9. entire

10. barley

Spelling

11. ______________

12. ______________

13. ______________

14. ______________

15. ______________

Vocabulary

16. ______________

17. ______________

18. ______________

19. ______________

20. ______________

21. ______________

Alphabetizing

22. ________ why

________ wheat

________ what

________ were

________ whim

________ was

The Great Melting Pot

Have you heard people say that this country is the Great Melting Pot? What do you think that means? It means that though people come to live here from **all** over the world, they are all part of this country. It is like cooking a pot of soup. You might put in some meat, a carrot, some rice, and many other kinds of food. If you cook the soup for a long, long time, **everything** that you put into the pot blends together. When you eat the soup, it has one taste. It is not the taste of meat or carrot or rice. It is the taste of the soup! The soup has cooked long enough so that all the tastes blend into one. This country is like a big soup pot. Many people who live here now once lived somewhere else. This country has people who don't think the same. It has people who are not the same **color** or the same **religion,** but put them all together and they are one people. They blend into the people of this country. They do not forget their **traditions** or homelands, but they are all Americans. These things are all part of the great soup that is the Great Melting Pot of this country.

23. Do all people in this country come from the same place? ______________________

____

____

24. How are soup and this country the same? ______________________

____

____

25. What is the same for all the people of this country?

- ○ Their religion
- ○ Their color
- ○ Their thoughts
- ○ None of the above

26. Why is this country like a Great Melting Pot?

- ○ The people like meat, carrots, and rice.
- ○ The people are not the same but are still one people.
- ○ The people like it here.
- ○ None of the above

27. When people come here from another place, what do they forget?

- ○ Their homeland
- ○ Their religion
- ○ Their traditions
- ○ None of the above

all: ŏl **everything:** ĕv′ rē thĭng **color:** kəl′ er **religion:** rĭ lĭj′ ən **traditions:** trə dĭsh′ əns

Name ______________________________

Teacher's Initials _____

Assessment 14
Phonics Intervention
(Give anytime after Lesson 84)

Coding and Reading

1. amount
2. divide
3. evicted
4. provide
5. superb
6. smallest
7. closet
8. illness
9. portion
10. swap

Spelling

11. ______________
12. ______________
13. ______________
14. ______________
15. ______________

Vocabulary

16. ______________
17. ______________
18. ______________
19. ______________
20. ______________
21. ______________

Alphabetizing

22. stock ______________ straight

The Bill of Rights

Since the Constitution was written, we have been able to adapt it to fit the times. **Lawmakers** can add to it or make changes called "amendments." The three **voting**-rights amendments are good examples of this. The first voting-rights amendment was the Fifteenth Amendment, which gave the vote to black men. Then the Nineteenth Amendment gave women the same right. The last is the Twenty-sixth Amendment, which lowered the voting age from 21 to 18. The most important amendments were the first ten. Without them, there would be no Constitution. Four states would not **agree** to sign the Constitution without these amendments, known as the Bill of Rights. The Bill of Rights protects the rights of the **individual.** The first two rights are the right to free speech and the right of people to get together and ask the **government** to make changes. Without these rights, Martin Luther King, Jr. could not have led his march on Washington. The main **promise** of the Bill of Rights is that the government will listen to the people and protect their right to speak out for what they think is right.

23. What is an amendment to the Constitution? ______________________________

____

____

24. What is the name of the first ten amendments to the Constitution? ____________

____

____

25. What does the Bill of Rights promise us?

- ○ To allow women to vote
- ○ To give black men the vote
- ○ To protect the rights of the individual
- ○ None of the above

26. What amendment to the Constitution gives women the right to vote?

- ○ First Amendment
- ○ Twenty-sixth Amendment
- ○ Fifteenth Amendment
- ○ None of the above

27. What did the Twenty-sixth Amendment to the Constitution do?

- ○ Lowered the voting age from 21 to 18
- ○ Gave Martin Luther King, Jr. the right to march on Washington
- ○ Gave people the right of free speech
- ○ None of the above

lawmakers: lŏ′ mā kerz **voting:** vōt′ ĭng **agree:** ə grē′
individual: ĭn də vĭj′ wəl **government:** gəv′ ern mənt **promise:** prŏ′ məs

ASSESSMENTS

Name ______________________________

Teacher's Initials ______

Assessment 15
Phonics Intervention
(Give anytime after Lesson 90)

Coding and Reading

1. lie
2. piece
3. protein
4. vein
5. wonder
6. mildew
7. launch
8. shawl
9. London
10. charcoal

Spelling

11. ______________
12. ______________
13. ______________
14. ______________
15. ______________

Vocabulary

16. ______________
17. ______________
18. ______________
19. ______________
20. ______________
21. ______________

Alphabetizing

22. mount moth mouse more miss

____

____

____

____

____

ASSESSMENTS

The White House

The most **famous** address in the United States is 1600 **Pennsylvania** Avenue, Washington, D.C. It is the address of the White House, the home of the president. The White House was planned by James **Hoban,** who won a contest held to choose the best **design.** He drew up plans for a beautiful white house with a wide lawn around it. President Washington laid the cornerstone in 1792, and the building was completed in 1808. John Adams was the first president to live there. Congress gave his wife, Abigail, money to buy things for the house. Since then, every president's wife has added her own special **touches.** A lot happens at the White House. Dinners are given for important guests from other **countries.** Special events are held on the lawn. The president often speaks to the American people from his **office** in the White House. The White House does not belong to any president. It belongs to the American people.

23. Who lives in the White House? ______________________________

____

____

24. In what city is the White House found? ______________________________

____

____

25. How was James Hoban selected to design the White House?

- ○ John Adams chose him.
- ○ He won a contest.
- ○ Abigail Adams chose him.
- ○ None of the above

26. In what year was the White House completed?

- ○ 1600
- ○ 1808
- ○ 1792
- ○ None of the above

27. To whom does the White House belong?

- ○ The president
- ○ Congress
- ○ The American people
- ○ None of the above

famous: fā′ məs **Pennsylvania:** pĕn səl vā′ nyə **Hoban:** hō′ bən
design: dĭ zīn′ **touches:** təch′ ĕz **countries:** kən′ trēz **office:** ŏf′ əs

Name ______________________________

Teacher's Initials ______

Assessment 16

Phonics Intervention

(Give anytime after Lesson 96)

Coding and Reading

1. hatches
2. preshrunk
3. overflow
4. underage
5. rodeo
6. clever
7. skillful
8. monkey
9. fitness
10. fraud

Spelling

11. ______________
12. ______________
13. ______________
14. ______________
15. ______________

Vocabulary

16. ______________
17. ______________
18. ______________
19. ______________
20. ______________
21. ______________

Alphabetizing

22. gilt

ginger • glad

____

ASSESSMENTS

The City of New York

New York is a city always in motion. It has undergound trains called "subways." The streets and sidewalks are alive with people and traffic. From the top of the Empire State Building, you get a great **view** of the city. When you come down, you can visit one of New York City's many museums, relax in Central Park, or window shop along Fifth Avenue. At nightfall you can see a **Broadway** play, dine in a beautiful **restaurant,** listen to music, or look at the neon lights in Times Square. New York City has a rich history. It was founded by the Dutch in the early 1600s. They called it "New Amsterdam." In 1664, England took over the city and changed its name to "New York." Many historic events have taken place in New York City; for example, George Washington took the oath as first president of the U.S. here. New York City was this country's first Melting Pot. It was here that people who moved to America from all over the world first came. They got their first look at the Statue of Liberty in New York Harbor. The newcomers left their mark on New York City's **neighborhoods.** There you can hear many **languages,** eat foods from many **countries,** and enjoy festivals **celebrating** many cultures. No wonder there is a song that says "New York, New York's a wonderful town."

23. Who founded the city we now call New York? ______________________________

____

24. When was the city founded? ______________________________

____

25. What name did the Dutch give New York City?

- ○ New York, New York
- ○ New Amsterdam
- ○ Hudson City
- ○ None of the above

26. What historic event happened in New York City?

- ○ They put neon lights in Times Square.
- ○ It was the country's first Melting Pot.
- ○ George Washington took the oath of office as first president of the U.S.
- ○ None of the above

27. What helps make New York the special place that it is?

- ○ The people from other countries
- ○ The many zoos and museums
- ○ The Broadway shows and restaurants
- ○ All of the above

view: vyū **Broadway:** brŏd′ wā **restaurant:** res′ tə rənt
neighborhoods: nā′ ber hŏŏdz **languages:** lăn′ gwĭj ĕz
countries: kən′ trēz **celebrating:** sĕl′ ə brāt ĭng

Name ______________________________

Teacher's Initials ______

Assessment 17
Phonics Intervention
(Give anytime after Lesson 100)

Coding and Reading

1. transfusion
2. discussion
3. capture
4. distrust
5. selfish
6. insane
7. unsafe
8. delicious
9. artist
10. sharpen

Spelling

11. ______________
12. ______________
13. ______________
14. ______________
15. ______________

Vocabulary

16. ______________
17. ______________
18. ______________
19. ______________
20. ______________
21. ______________

Alphabetizing

22. leave

______________ • ______________

ASSESSMENTS

America the Beautiful

There is a famous song about this country called "America the Beautiful." It praises the **beauties** of this country from "sea to shining sea." Its words tell of America's great plains, its wide fields of grain, and the majesty of its mountains. One of the most famous mountain ranges in the United States is the Rocky Mountains. These mountains, often called the "Rockies," are located west of the Mississippi River. They extend from north to south for 3,000 miles from Canada into New Mexico. The Rockies are part of what is known as the Continental Divide. All the rivers east of the Continental Divide flow toward the Atlantic Ocean. All the rivers west of the Continental Divide flow toward the Pacific Ocean. The Rockies have many centers for camping and **tourism.** Yellowstone National Park, the first of our national parks, is located in the Rockies. Yellowstone's almost 3,500 square miles of land was set aside as a national park in 1872. It is a symbol of the beauty of our country and our pledge to preserve its natural beauty. America is beautiful. It is our duty to preserve this land because in the words of another famous song, "this land was made for you and me."

23. How far do the Rockies extend from north to south? ______________________

____

____

24. When was Yellowstone made a National Park? ______________________

____

____

25. Where do the rivers west of the Continental Divide flow?

- ○ Toward the Atlantic Ocean
- ○ Toward the Pacific Ocean
- ○ Toward the Mississippi River
- ○ None of the above

26. How large is Yellowstone National Park?

- ○ Almost 1,804 square miles
- ○ Almost 3,000 square miles
- ○ Almost 3,500 square miles
- ○ None of the above

27. Why is it important to preserve America's natural beauty?

- ○ To build national parks
- ○ So people can write songs about it
- ○ Because this land was made for you and me
- ○ None of the above

beauties: byū´ tēz **tourism:** tŭr´ ĭ zəm

Name ______________________________

Teacher's Initials ______

Vocabulary Test 1
Phonics Intervention
(Give anytime after Lesson 20)

Section 1: Definitions

alp ban damp lag dim fib jot nod hum pun

1. ______________

2. ______________

3. ______________

4. ______________

5. ______________

6. ______________

7. ______________

8. ______________

9. ______________

10. ______________

Name ________________________________

Teacher's Initials ______

Vocabulary Test 2

Phonics Intervention

(Give anytime after Lesson 30)

Section 1: Definitions

text clasp pry myth dash chat con wick indent pang

1. ____________ **5.** ____________ **9.** ____________

2. ____________ **6.** ____________ **10.** ____________

3. ____________ **7.** ____________

4. ____________ **8.** ____________

Section 2: Sentence Completion

alp ban damp lag dim fib jot nod hum pun

11. Don't __________ behind or you might get separated from the group.

12. His __________, or play on words, was extremely funny!

13. My grandmother likes to __________ along while my grandfather plays his guitar.

14. The light was __________, and we had to walk slowly so that we would not knock anything over.

15. How many days will it take us to climb the __________?

16. Please __________ down the names of everyone who will be coming to the birthday party.

17. Many people have tried to __________ that book but have been unsuccessful.

18. The clothes were still __________, so I put them back in the dryer.

19. If you tell a __________, it will usually catch up with you.

20. His mouth was so swollen that he had to __________ his head when he wanted something instead of talking.

Name ______________________________

Teacher's Initials ______

Vocabulary Test 3

Phonics Intervention

(Give anytime after Lesson 40)

Section 1: Definitions

pride seize stray sneer verb shirk murmur quest whim stumps

1. ______________ **5.** ______________ **9.** ______________

2. ______________ **6.** ______________ **10.** ______________

3. ______________ **7.** ______________

4. ______________ **8.** ______________

Section 2: Sentence Completion

text clasp pry myth dash chat con wick indent pang

11. The candle __________ was so short that I could not light it.

12. Don't forget to __________ each paragraph on your final report.

13. He was a __________ artist; he tricked us into giving him our coats.

14. This recipe calls for a __________ of cinnamon; would you __________ to the store and buy some for me?

15. Was Paul Bunyan a __________ or was he real?

16. Please read the __________ carefully before answering the questions.

17. Can you __________ that greasy bone from the dog's mouth so she won't get sick?

18. My uncle broke the __________ on his watch.

19. Shantray likes to get on the Internet and __________ with friends all over the world.

20. I felt a sharp __________ when I remembered that I had forgotten to call my mother as I had promised.

Section 3: Writing Sentences

alp ban damp lag dim fib jot nod hum pun

21. ______________________________

22. ______________________________

23. ______________________________

24. ______________________________

25. ______________________________

26. ______________________________

27. ______________________________

28. ______________________________

29. ______________________________

30. ______________________________

Name ______________________________

Teacher's Initials ______

Vocabulary Test 4
Phonics Intervention
(Give anytime after Lesson 50)

Section 1: Definitions

sifting basked pact marsh border vendor collards fossil dusk proof

1. ______________ **5.** ______________ **9.** ______________

2. ______________ **6.** ______________ **10.** ______________

3. ______________ **7.** ______________

4. ______________ **8.** ______________

Section 2: Sentence Completion

pride seize stray sneer verb shirk murmur quest whim stumps

11. Mr. Black always has at least one question on his history tests that ____________ me.

12. My mom likes to tell me not to ____________ my duty as a family member and take out the trash.

13. If your teacher hears you ____________ during a test, he or she might think you are cheating.

14. My little sister is on a ____________ to find gold in our backyard.

15. We decided to go to the movies on a ____________, but we should have stayed home because the movie was terrible.

16. In the sentence "The fat cat sat outside," "sat" is the ____________.

17. The ____________ in her face was obvious when her son sang his solo.

18. The ____________ cat was cold and hungry, so we brought him inside and fed him some milk.

19. When I saw the ____________ on his face, I knew it was time to separate the two boys.

20. We should ____________ the moment when opportunities arise because they may not come again.

VOCABULARY TESTS

Section 3: Writing Sentences

text clasp pry myth dash chat con wick indent pang

21. ______

22. ______

23. ______

24. ______

25. ______

26. ______

27. ______

28. ______

29. ______

30. ______

Section 4: Writing Definitions

31. alp: ______________________________

____

32. ban: ______________________________

____

33. damp: ______________________________

____

34. lag: ______________________________

____

35. dim: ______________________________

____

36. fib: ______________________________

____

37. jot: ______________________________

____

38. nod: ______________________________

____

39. hum: ______________________________

____

40. pun: ______________________________

____

Name ______________________________

Teacher's Initials ______

Vocabulary Test 5

Phonics Intervention

(Give anytime after Lesson 60)

Section 1: Definitions

rind spur stocker scuff fable ladle trifle graph solve deaf

1. ________________ **5.** ________________ **9.** ________________

2. ________________ **6.** ________________ **10.** ________________

3. ________________ **7.** ________________

4. ________________ **8.** ________________

Section 2: Sentence Completion

sifting basked pact marsh border vendor collards fossil dusk proof

11. The hogs ____________ in the sun after eating the Thanksgiving leftovers.

12. Riley and his teacher made a __________ with each other that he would do his homework every night.

13. Marcos was ____________ through the trash looking for his retainer.

14. The ____________ was full of cattails and tall grass.

15. At __________ we went outside to play a quick game of "Capture the Flag."

16. The ____________ around the print was blue to match the water in the picture.

17. Maria and Jason ate the _____________, but no one else would even touch them.

18. In Washington, D.C., there is always a ____________ selling water and fruit outside the Smithsonian Museum.

19. His movie ticket was ___________ that he had been at the movies and not at school.

20. The rock was very old and contained a ___________ of a dinosaur footprint.

Section 3: Writing Sentences

pride seize stray sneer verb shirk murmur quest whim stumps

21. ______________________________

____

22. ______________________________

____

23. ______________________________

____

24. ______________________________

____

25. ______________________________

____

26. ______________________________

____

27. ______________________________

____

28. ______________________________

____

29. ______________________________

____

30. ______________________________

____

Section 4: Writing Definitions

31. text: ______________________________

32. clasp: ______________________________

33. pry: ______________________________

34. myth: ______________________________

35. dash: ______________________________

36. chat: ______________________________

37. con: ______________________________

38. wick: ______________________________

39. indent: ______________________________

40. pang: ______________________________

Section 5: Matching

41. alp	__________	A. to write down something quickly
42. ban	__________	B. to sing with lips closed
43. damp	__________	C. not bright; unclear
44. lag	__________	D. move the head up and down in agreement
45. dim	__________	E. to fall behind
46. fib	__________	F. a high, rugged mountain
47. jot	__________	G. a play on words
48. nod	__________	H. to prohibit or forbid
49. hum	__________	I. a childish lie
50. pun	__________	J. a little wet

Name ______________________________

Teacher's Initials ______

Vocabulary Test 6
Phonics Intervention
(Give anytime after Lesson 70)

Section 1: Definitions

flimsy kneel trace douse stow hoist embargo sobbing employ sniffle

1. ______________ **5.** ______________ **9.** ______________

2. ______________ **6.** ______________ **10.** ______________

3. ______________ **7.** ______________

4. ______________ **8.** ______________

Section 2: Sentence Completion

rind spur stocker scuff fable ladle trifle graph solve deaf

11. The ____________ showed that more students liked hamburgers than collard greens.

12. The grocery store ______________ was filling the shelves with canned carrots and peas.

13. Sierra was ___________, but she could read people's lips and talk using her hands.

14. The horse happily ate the watermelon __________ as if it were candy.

15. It was midnight, but Ling was going to study until she could ____________ every math problem easily.

16. Hunter gave Allison a necklace, which was a ____________ compared to the new sports car her parents gave her.

17. "Peter and the Wolf" is a very popular Russian ____________.

18. Jeannie tried not to ____________ her newly polished shoes before she left for the wedding.

19. We had to ___________ the group on to get them to finish cleaning out the attic.

20. The ____________ fell in the hot soup, and I could not get it out without burning my fingers.

VOCABULARY TESTS

Section 3: Writing Sentences

sifting basked pact marsh border vendor collards fossil dusk proof

21. ______________________________

22. ______________________________

23. ______________________________

24. ______________________________

25. ______________________________

26. ______________________________

27. ______________________________

28. ______________________________

29. ______________________________

30. ______________________________

Section 4: Writing Definitions

31. pride: ______________________________

____

32. seize: ______________________________

____

33. stray: ______________________________

____

34. sneer: ______________________________

____

35. verb: ______________________________

____

36. shirk: ______________________________

____

37. murmur: ______________________________

____

38. quest: ______________________________

____

39. whim: ______________________________

____

40. stumps: ______________________________

____

Section 5: Matching

41. text	________	A. to open with difficulty
42. clasp	________	B. a light, relaxed conversation
43. pry	________	C. to space in from the margin
44. myth	________	D. the printed words on a page
45. dash	________	E. a legendary or imaginary story
46. chat	________	F. to swindle or trick
47. con	________	G. a quick, short pain or feeling
48. wick	________	H. to hold something tightly
49. indent	________	I. a small amount
50. pang	________	J. the string that burns in a candle

Name ______________________________

Teacher's Initials ______

Vocabulary Test 7

Phonics Intervention

(Give anytime after Lesson 80)

Section 1: Definitions

gist duty weekly plight notch sludge wage gulch motion river

1. ______________ **5.** ______________ **9.** ______________

2. ______________ **6.** ______________ **10.** ______________

3. ______________ **7.** ______________

4. ______________ **8.** ______________

Section 2: Sentence Completion

flimsy kneel trace douse stow hoist embargo sobbing employ sniffle

11. The ______________ on oil made the price of gasoline soar.

12. The children were ______________ until their lost kitten was found.

13. We will ______________ the Christmas ornaments in the attic until next year.

14. Please ______________ the campfire before you leave the camping area.

15. The new store will ______________ about one hundred people.

16. We had to ______________ the piano up the stairs with a rope in order to get it to the fifth floor of the apartment.

17. The recipe calls for a ______________ of salt, which isn't very much.

18. The hot dog fell off the ______________ paper plate right into the mouth of the expectant puppy.

19. In the play, we had to ______________ down and pretend that Ryan was a king.

20. We heard a ______________ behind the clothes rack and found a lost child.

Section 3: Writing Sentences

(Vocabulary Test 7, continued)

rind spur stocker scuff fable ladle trifle graph solve deaf

21. ______________________________

22. ______________________________

23. ______________________________

24. ______________________________

25. ______________________________

26. ______________________________

27. ______________________________

28. ______________________________

29. ______________________________

30. ______________________________

VOCABULARY TESTS

Section 4: Writing Definitions

31. sifting: ______________________________

____

32. basked: ______________________________

____

33. pact: ______________________________

____

34. marsh: ______________________________

____

35. border: ______________________________

____

36. vendor: ______________________________

____

37. collards: ______________________________

____

38. fossil: ______________________________

____

39. dusk: ______________________________

____

40. proof: ______________________________

____

Section 5: Matching

41. pride __________	A. a lost animal
42. seize __________	B. to speak in a low voice
43. stray __________	C. stubs of main parts; presents a problem no one can answer
44. sneer __________	D. pleasure in one's person or possessions
45. verb __________	E. urge to do something for no particular reason
46. shirk __________	F. to grab hold of; to snatch
47. murmur __________	G. a search for something valuable
48. quest __________	H. a facial expression showing dislike or scorn
49. whim __________	I. to avoid doing a job that should be done
50. stumps __________	J. word that shows action or condition

Name ______________________________

Teacher's Initials ______

Vocabulary Test 8
Phonics Intervention
(Give anytime after Lesson 90)

Section 1: Definitions

waltz unite adapt coding auction crew ton rein grateful museum

1. ______________ **5.** ______________ **9.** ______________

2. ______________ **6.** ______________ **10.** ______________

3. ______________ **7.** ______________

4. ______________ **8.** ______________

Section 2: Sentence Completion

gist duty weekly plight notch sludge wage gulch motion river

11. He received a __________ of one hundred fifty dollars every Thursday.

12. I take lessons __________ so I can become a better piano player.

13. The Nile is the longest __________ in the world, although the Amazon contains more water.

14. We tried to find a new way down the mountain but ran into a __________ that we could not cross.

15. Keeping my room clean seemed to be the __________ of the lecture from my father.

16. Keeley made the __________ to vote on the new rules for the classroom.

17. It is our __________ as citizens of this country to obey the law.

18. We cleaned the __________ out of the hot water heater before filling it up with water again.

19. Anton carved a __________ on his bat every time he hit a home run.

20. People all over the world sympathized with the victims' __________ and sent in food and money to help.

Section 3: Writing Sentences

flimsy kneel trace douse stow hoist embargo sobbing employ sniffle

21. ______________________________

22. ______________________________

23. ______________________________

24. ______________________________

25. ______________________________

26. ______________________________

27. ______________________________

28. ______________________________

29. ______________________________

30. ______________________________

Section 4: Writing Definitions

31. rind: ______________________________

32. spur: ______________________________

33. stocker: ______________________________

34. scuff: ______________________________

35. fable: ______________________________

36. ladle: ______________________________

37. trifle: ______________________________

38. graph: ______________________________

39. solve: ______________________________

40. deaf: ______________________________

41. sifting ____________

42. basked ____________

43. pact ____________

44. marsh ____________

45. border ____________

46. vendor ____________

47. collards ____________

48. fossil ____________

49. dusk ____________

50. proof ____________

A. late evening just before dark

B. one who sells

C. something used to show correctness or truth

D. a print or trace of an animal or plant that lived long ago

E. the leaves of a type of cabbage

F. took pleasure in; enjoyed a pleasant warmth

G. an edge or margin

H. a swampy area

I. straining something to separate the larger pieces from the smaller ones

J. an agreement or contract between people or countries

Name ____

Teacher's Initials _____

Vocabulary Test 9
Phonics Intervention
(Give anytime after Lesson 100)

Section 1: Definitions

prefix suffixes rustic version disinfect infectious unselfish rebelling hydrant fragile

1. ________________ **5.** ________________ **9.** ________________

2. ________________ **6.** ________________ **10.** ________________

3. ________________ **7.** ________________

4. ________________ **8.** ________________

Section 2: Sentence Completion

waltz unite adapt coding auction crew ton rein grateful museum

11. The books seemed to weigh a __________ as the students moved shelf after shelf into the new library.

12. As the ____________ played, Validia dreamed of dancing with Esteban.

13. Many animals must ____________ to the cold or migrate south for the winter where it is warmer.

14. Cynthia was great at _____________ words, but she had difficulty putting the syllables together to read the words.

15. Jermal held an ______________ every weekend for six months and sold hundreds of items to customers.

16. The road ____________ began sanding the roads as soon as the snow started to fall.

17. The Republicans will have to ____________ with the Democrats for the good of the country.

18. The horse's ___________ was so thin that it seemed the horse could break free easily.

19. Patrick was very _______________ when Sean agreed to help him study for his science test.

20. Our class is going to the ________________ tomorrow morning to see the dinosaur fossils.

Section 3: Writing Sentences

gist duty weekly plight notch sludge wage gulch motion river

21. ______________________________

22. ______________________________

23. ______________________________

24. ______________________________

25. ______________________________

26. ______________________________

27. ______________________________

28. ______________________________

29. ______________________________

30. ______________________________

Section 4: Writing Definitions

31. flimsy: ______________________________

____

32. kneel: ______________________________

____

33. trace: ______________________________

____

____

34. douse: ______________________________

____

35. stow: ______________________________

____

36. hoist: ______________________________

____

37. embargo: ______________________________

____

38. sobbing: ______________________________

____

39. employ: ______________________________

____

40. sniffle: ______________________________

____

Section 5: Matching

41. rind __________

42. spur __________

43. stocker __________

44. scuff __________

45. fable __________

46. ladle __________

47. trifle __________

48. graph __________

49. solve __________

50. deaf __________

A. a metal piece on the heel of a rider's boot

B. a chart that shows the relationship between things

C. to find an explanation for or answer to

D. a short story that teaches a lesson

E. a tough outer covering like the peeling on fruit

F. something that is unimportant; a small amount

G. to scratch up the surface; to shuffle when walking

H. not able to hear

I. one who keeps the supplies on the shelves

J. a serving spoon that looks like a cup with a long handle

Name ______________________________

Teacher's Initials ______

Final Vocabulary Test
Phonics Intervention
(Give anytime after Vocabulary Test 9)

1. fib ____________ A. to rest on one or both knees

2. whim ____________ B. a childish lie

3. kneel ____________ C. to store for future use

4. stow ____________ D. urge to do something for no particular reason

---

5. jot ____________ E. a team of people working together

6. stumps ____________ F. to write something down quickly

7. trace ____________ G. stubs of main parts; presents a problem no one can answer

8. crew ____________ H. to copy a picture on see-through paper; a very small amount

---

9. wick ____________ I. a tough outer covering like the peeling on fruit

10. rind ____________ J. an unfortunate, difficult situation

11. plight ____________ K. not stingy

12. unselfish ____________ L. the string that burns in a candle

---

13. indent ____________ M. fighting against authority

14. spur ____________ N. a v-shaped cut

15. notch ____________ O. a metal piece on the heel of a rider's boot

16. rebelling ____________ P. to space in from the margin

17. dim	______	Q. a search for something valuable
18. quest	______	R. marking a word with sound symbols
19. flimsy	______	S. not bright; unclear
20. coding	______	T. thin, easily damaged
21. nod	______	U. to cover completely with liquid
22. sifting	______	V. 2000 pounds
23. douse	______	W. move the head up and down in agreement
24. ton	______	X. using a sieve
25. con	______	Y. once every week
26. proof	______	Z. to swindle or trick
27. weekly	______	A. capable of spreading disease
28. infectious	______	B. something used to show the truth
29. pang	______	C. a large pipe-like water faucet on the curb
30. stocker	______	D. a quick, short pain or feeling
31. sludge	______	E. one who keeps the supplies on the shelves
32. hydrant	______	F. slimy waste material

33. lag	__________	G.	to speak in a low voice
34. murmur	__________	H.	not able to hear
35. deaf	__________	I.	to make fit for a certain use
36. adapt	__________	J.	to fall behind

---

37. hum	__________	K.	a leather strap attached to a horse's bit
38. basked	__________	L.	to store for future use
39. stow	__________	M.	took pleasure in; enjoyed a pleasant warmth
40. rein	__________	N.	to sing with lips closed

---

41. chat	__________	O.	late evening just before dark
42. dusk	__________	P.	to cleanse to kill disease germs
43. duty	__________	Q.	a light, relaxed conversation
44. disinfect	__________	R.	something a person must do

---

45. pride	__________	S.	money paid to an employee for work done
46. scuff	__________	T.	not strong; easily broken
47. wage	__________	U.	pleasure in one's person or possessions
48. fragile	__________	V.	to scratch up the surface; to shuffle when walking

49. damp	____________	W. to find an explanation for or answer to
50. shirk	____________	X. a little wet
51. solve	____________	Y. to bring together for a common purpose
52. unite	____________	Z. to avoid doing a job that should be done

---

53. pun	____________	A. thankful; appreciative
54. pact	____________	B. a play on words
55. hoist	____________	C. an agreement or contract between people or countries
56. grateful	____________	D. to lift into position with a pulley or rope

---

57. dash	____________	E. a print or trace of an animal or plant that lived long ago
58. fossil	____________	F. the main idea
59. gist	____________	G. a report from one point of view
60. version	____________	H. a small amount

---

61. seize	____________	I. three letters that come together to make one sound
62. fable	____________	J. a deep, narrow ravine
63. gulch	____________	K. a short story that teaches a lesson
64. trigraph	____________	L. to grab hold of; to snatch

65. ban	____________	M.	word that shows action or condition
66. verb	____________	N.	a ballroom dance for couples
67. graph	____________	O.	to prohibit or forbid
68. waltz	____________	P.	a chart that shows the relationship between things

---

69. text	____________	Q.	a government restriction on trade or shipping ports
70. marsh	____________	R.	a building in which important objects are displayed
71. embargo	____________	S.	the printed words on a page
72. museum	____________	T.	a swampy area

---

73. myth	____________	U.	to cry a little
74. collards	____________	V.	a legendary or imaginary story
75. sniffle	____________	W.	plain, simple, and natural
76. rustic	____________	X.	the leaves of a type of cabbage

---

77. stray	____________	Y.	plentiful; more than is needed
78. ladle	____________	Z.	a lost animal
79. motion	____________	A.	a serving spoon that looks like a cup with a long handle
80. bountiful	____________	B.	the action of moving; a formal request in a meeting

81. alp	______	C.	a facial expression showing dislike or scorn
82. sneer	______	D.	something that is unimportant; a small amount
83. trifle	______	E.	a large, natural stream
84. river	______	F.	a high, rugged mountain

---

85. clasp	______	G.	letters added to the beginning of a word
86. border	______	H.	crying aloud
87. sobbing	______	I.	an edge or margin
88. prefix	______	J.	to hold something tightly

---

89. pry	______	K.	put to work; hire
90. vendor	______	L.	letters added to the ends of root words
91. employ	______	M.	to open with difficulty
92. suffixes	______	N.	one who sells

Name ______________________________

Teacher's Initials ______

Speed Drill 1
Phonics Intervention
(Give anytime after Lesson 14)

Date	Time	Name of Timer

1. are
2. from
3. of
4. said
5. to
6. want
7. was
8. were
9. what
10. where

1. to
2. was
3. what
4. are
5. of
6. said
7. want
8. were
9. where
10. from

1. Where are the gifts?

2. What is that mess?

3. Was the box red?

4. Go to Pam's and get the fish net.

5. I want a dog.

6. Is the gift from Dad?

7. It is a box of gum.

8. Mom said it was on the desk.

9. The golf clubs were in the shed.

Name ______________________________

Teacher's Initials ______

Speed Drill 2
Phonics Intervention
(Give anytime after Lesson 21)

1. come
2. didn't
3. do
4. does
5. don't
6. one
7. put
8. says
9. some
10. who

1. says
2. put
3. don't
4. do
5. didn't
6. who
7. some
8. one
9. does
10. come

Date	Time	Name of Timer

"Come here!" says Max. "Who put the milk on the shelf and let it spill?"

"I didn't spill the milk," says Jan, "but don't we need to clean some of it up?"

"No," says Max. "I think Glen made the mess, so he must do it."

"Glen is not home, so he didn't make the mess," says Jan.

"Well, if we didn't make the mess, and Glen didn't make the mess, does that mean the cat made the mess?" asks Jan.

"Yes," says Max. "That must be the case. I think the cat was the one who made the mess."

Name ____________________

Teacher's Initials ______

Speed Drill 3
Phonics Intervention
(Give anytime after Lesson 31)

1. because	**1.** they
2. been	**2.** their
3. could	**3.** other
4. four	**4.** four
5. other	**5.** been
6. should	**6.** would
7. their	**7.** there
8. there	**8.** should
9. they	**9.** because
10. would	**10.** could

Date	Time	Name of Timer

"We should not be here because Rob and Lynn need help," said Tim. "Their four dogs—Bandit, Max, Kate, and Tramp—are missing."

"Was the gate shut?" asked Jo.

"Yes, but Tramp and one of the other dogs like to dig holes," said Tim.

"Would Rob and Lynn hunt for their dogs if they were lost?" asked Jo.

"Yes, they would because the dogs could get hit on the street. Their dogs mean a lot to them, so we should see if they need help. Rob and Lynn would help us if we needed them," said Tim.

"The dogs **have** (hăv) been lost a long time, so let's go there and see if we can spot them!" said Jo.

Name ______________________________

Teacher's Initials ______

Speed Drill 4
Phonics Intervention
(Give anytime after Lesson 37)

1. any	**1.** sure
2. brother	**2.** mother
3. buy	**3.** learn
4. father	**4.** buy
5. learn	**5.** any
6. many	**6.** trouble
7. mother	**7.** ocean
8. ocean	**8.** many
9. sure	**9.** father
10. trouble	**10.** brother

Date	Time	Name of Timer

Many come to the coast to see the ocean and to sun on the beach. While there, they learn that it is best to leave their troubles at home so they can rest. My father, mother, brother, and I work in a gift shop on the beach. Shoppers buy many things from the four of us. Mother makes sure to assist them anytime they need help. My brother collects shells on the beach for them to buy. My father likes to fish in the ocean and help anyone who gets in trouble in the big waves. Anyone who comes to the ocean learns something. My father and mother are sure that my brother and I will want to stay here for many years.

Name ____________________

Teacher's Initials ______

Speed Drill 5
Phonics Intervention
(Give anytime after Lesson 43)

1. again (against)	1. walk
2. door	2. only
3. enough	3. give (live)
4. friend	4. enough
5. give (live)	5. again (against)
6. have	6. young
7. only	7. talk
8. talk	8. have
9. walk	9. friend
10. young	10. door

Date	Time	Name of Timer

When I was young, I had a best friend who was the best friend in the whole world. When I walked in the door at school, she would give me a big smile, and after school we would go walk and talk by the ocean. When we had troubles, we would talk for a long time. My friend was the only other girl in my class. I was so glad she sat by me. No other friend could have been better than she. Many years have passed and we are much older. We no longer have homes in the same state. My friend and I don't get to walk and talk like we used to do. Sometimes I dream of being young again. I wish my friend lived close enough so that we could take walks like we did back then.

Name ______________________________

Teacher's Initials ______

Speed Drill 6
Phonics Intervention
(Give anytime after Lesson 49)

1. country
2. early
3. earth
4. eye
5. fought
6. heard
7. two
8. whose
9. woman
10. women

1. woman
2. two
3. fought
4. earth
5. country
6. women
7. whose
8. heard
9. eye
10. early

Date	Time	Name of Timer

I have heard from my grandfather that life in the early 1900s could be quite hard. He and his mother, father, brothers, and sisters lived in the country on a farm; they worked the earth to raise crops for food. If it didn't rain enough, there were no crops. Both women and men worked hard to raise food, but it could be trying at times. One time two of my grandfather's brothers fought, and one brother gave the other brother a black eye. A woman who lived close by, whose father was a doctor, ran to get help. In those days a simple cut could sometimes turn into something more grave. The doctor had to make sure that the man's eye did not get infected or he would not be able to see again.

Name ______________________________

Teacher's Initials ______

Speed Drill 7
Phonics Intervention
(Give anytime after Lesson 55)

1. cousin	**1.** gone
2. gone	**2.** guess (guest)
3. guard	**3.** island
4. guess (guest)	**4.** listen
5. half	**5.** once
6. island	**6.** mountain
7. laugh	**7.** laugh
8. listen	**8.** half
9. mountain	**9.** guard
10. once	**10.** cousin

Date	Time	Name of Timer

My cousin, Bruce, has been gone for ten years. He enlisted in the Air Force when he was twenty-two years old. I would guess that for half of his life Bruce had dreamed of flying. The Air Force base where he lived was on a splendid island at the base of a mountain. The base was set up there to guard the mainland. Seeing the airplanes top the mountain and cross the ocean waves as they came in for their landings was a true thrill for him. When Bruce went on trips, he **loved** (lŭvd) to listen to the roar of the plane when it took off. The feeling he got when the plane dipped made him laugh. Once he learned to make the planes spin, he wanted to do it again and again. Bruce once performed as a guest at an air show. After two years, when the time came for Bruce to leave the Air Force, he chose to stay and help others learn to train as expert flyers too.

Name ______________________________________

Teacher's Initials ______

Speed Drill 8
Phonics Intervention
(Give anytime after Lesson 61)

1. bought
2. brought
3. busy
4. cough
5. done
6. rough
7. though
8. thought
9. through
10. tough

1. brought
2. cough
3. rough
4. thought
5. tough
6. through
7. though
8. done
9. busy
10. bought

Date	Time	Name of Timer

We are through for the day and what a day it has been! We treated mumps, **chicken** (chĭk′ ən) pox, sore throats, and many other childhood ailments. It seemed that each child who came in had a bad cough. We thought that we would get the cough too, though we take strides to keep our lungs tough. Some of us thought of going out for lunch, but it was too busy, so Jim bought hamburgers and brought them to us. We find that on rough days it is better to just tough it out and eat lunch at the office. We know that the day will not be done until we are through with each sick child. We pride ourselves on being able to find the root of each child's problem. Each child is then sent home with the hope that he or she will feel better soon. I guess this was just another tough day at a busy doctor's office.

Name ______________________________

Teacher's Initials ______

Speed Drill 9
Phonics Intervention
(Give anytime after Lesson 67)

1. certain	**1.** sign
2. climb	**2.** push
3. floor	**3.** move
4. move	**4.** floor
5. often	**5.** certain
6. push	**6.** tastes
7. shoe	**7.** shoe
8. sign	**8.** often
9. tastes	**9.** very
10. very	**10.** climb

Date	Time	Name of Timer

Last winter my father and I wanted to move to an older home. We found a very pretty house with a "For Sale" sign in the yard. Since the house was warm and cozy-looking, we bought it. We were certain it would be the perfect home, or so we thought. I chose the upstairs bedroom so I could climb the stairs each day. Little did I know that the steps had holes under the carpet in which my shoes would get stuck. The slanted floors were a problem too. We often had to push the beds and tables back into place. We tried buying duct tape to try to stick the beds and tables to the floor, but the tape would peel off. The sticky tape would get on our shoes, too, and pick up dead bugs and dirt. Two weeks after we moved in, the ugly fruit paper started to flake off the plaster. Chunks of the paper turned up in the meat loaf we served Uncle Elmer. He thought it was green pepper, though it must have tasted like plaster. We feel certain that the house will be in better shape soon, but in the meantime, we do not invite friends to our "perfect" house.

Name ________________________________

Teacher's Initials ______

Speed Drill 10

Phonics Intervention

(Give anytime after Lesson 73)

1. above	1. none
2. answer	2. above
3. build	3. heart
4. caught (taught)	4. clothes
5. clothes	5. build
6. February	6. answer
7. heart	7. caught (taught)
8. none	8. February
9. nothing	9. nothing
10. straight	10. straight

Date	Time	Name of Timer

My first date was one that I won't soon forget. Jason asked me to go to dinner and the "King of Hearts" dance at the Teen Center on February 14. My answer was "Yes, that would be fun!" Since I had nothing red to wear and none of my clothes were fancy enough for a dance, Mom let me buy a cute dress. Jason left early to help build the stage for the band and to run wires for the sound system. I went straight home after my flute class to get dressed. Dinner was excellent and the only way to describe the Teen Center is to say it was stunning. Red hearts filled the room and there were red-and-white ribbons above each door. Though loud, the band was very good too. It was a great night until I caught my shoe on some sound wires by the stage. The sound stopped at once and each person at the dance looked my way to see what had happened. I went straight to Jason, feeling hurt and flustered. Nothing could stop the flow of tears that followed. Jason was at a loss for words, but he did give me a big hug. I was too embarrassed to stay, so Jason took me home. Will Jason and I go out again? I will keep my fingers crossed.

Name ____

Teacher's Initials ______

Speed Drill 11
Phonics Intervention
(Give anytime after Lesson 79)

1. beautiful
2. Dr.
3. full
4. Mrs.
5. poor
6. prove
7. shoulder
8. special
9. stomach
10. sugar

1. Dr.
2. shoulder
3. sugar
4. prove
5. stomach
6. special
7. poor
8. Mrs.
9. full
10. beautiful

Date	Time	Name of Timer

Once there was a beautiful girl, Ming, whose heart was full of good will. Her goal in life was to help children. She set out to prove that the way children are treated affects their outlook on life. Thus, she made it a point to see certain children every day. She would see sad children and children in poor health. Mrs. Crowley's five-year-old had chronic stomach problems that kept her in constant pain if she ate sugar. Dr. Lefler's son had a hard time in school. Others had special problems and simply needed a shoulder to cry on. Ming made each child feel special by spending time with him or her or helping the children with schoolwork. Before long, people began to see a difference. The children seemed to have more confidence, they appeared to feel better, they smiled more often, and they began to try to help their other friends. Ming was very happy to see that she had indeed made a difference in the children's lives. She wanted the children to have better lives due to her efforts.

Name ______________________________

Teacher's Initials ______

Speed Drill 12
Phonics Intervention
(Give anytime after Lesson 85)

1. aunt	**1.** Wednesday
2. course	**2.** pull
3. daughter	**3.** Ms.
4. hour	**4.** hour
5. Mr.	**5.** course
6. Ms.	**6.** aunt
7. pour	**7.** daughter
8. pull	**8.** Mr.
9. touch	**9.** pour
10. Wednesday	**10.** touch

Date	Time	Name of Timer

Last Wednesday morning, Mr. Sanders had one hour before he had to be at work. He wanted to relax a few moments before leaving his house, so he poured himself and Ms. Sanders two cups of coffee and then pulled up a chair to the kitchen table. He wanted to discuss a problem regarding his aunt and her daughter, Robin. Mr. Sanders had to touch Ms. Sanders' elbow to get her attention. It startled Ms. Sanders so much that she poured her coffee into her own lap. She jumped up and said, "You are going to be late for work!" Mr. Sanders replied, "I still have about an hour before I have to be there. On Wednesdays, I don't have to arrive until nine or ten a.m. Would you like for me to pour you some more coffee?" Ms. Sanders answered, "I think I have had enough. Of course, most of the coffee I made is in my lap now anyway." Mr. Sanders offered to make more coffee, but Ms. Sanders kindly responded, "No, thanks." Mr. Sanders thought he should wait until supper to discuss his problem with his aunt. He pulled his chair away from the table, trying not to touch or spill anything else. Mr. Sanders then left for work that Wednesday at eight rather than waiting until nine or ten.

Vocabulary List

(Alphabetized)

abolished did away with completely

adapt to change to make fit for a certain use

alp a high, rugged mountain

ambitious working hard to be successful

American colonies/colonists the first settlements in America/the first settlers

appointed chosen to serve and placed in a position or office

archives collections of historical records and documents

arena an enclosed area used for sports and other events

auction a public sale where goods are sold to the highest bidder

ban to prohibit or forbid

basked took pleasure in; enjoyed a pleasant warmth

baton a stick or rod used by a leader to direct

battle a fight in a war

bill a proposed law

border 1. an edge or margin; 2. the line or boundary where one thing ends and another begins

bountiful plentiful; more than is needed

Broadway a famous street in New York known for its theaters

capital the city where the governing bodies are located

center of trade the key place for buyers and sellers

chat a light, relaxed conversation

check a control or test

citizen a resident with legal rights and protection

civil rights the equal rights of all citizens (right to liberty and freedom)

clasp 1. a fastener to hold things together; 2. to hold something tightly, like to hold hands

coding marking a word with symbols to give information about how to pronounce it

collards the leaves of a type of cabbage, eaten as a vegetable

committee a group of people assigned a certain job to do

compiled brought together into one

con to swindle or trick

Continental Divide the north-to-south mountain ranges of the Rockies that divide the U.S. into east and west river flows

copper a soft, reddish metal that is easy to shape

cornerstone a special stone laid in the foundation of a building at one of its corners when it is being built

country a nation or state

courage the quality of standing against danger or hardship; being brave

court a group who decides issues of law

crew a team of people working together

damp a little wet

dash 1. to run quickly; 2. a small amount

dawn the beginning light of day

deaf not able to hear

Declaration of Independence the document that declared America was free from England

defeated won over another, as in war

dim not bright; unclear

disinfect to cleanse so as to kill disease germs

district one section of an area that has been divided up for a certain purpose

dome the rounded top of a building

douse 1. to cover completely with liquid; to drench; 2. to put out (a light or fire)

dusk late evening just before dark

duty 1. something a person must do; 2. a government tax on imported goods

earthquake a shaking or trembling of the earth that occurs when the ground moves because of shifting rocks beneath the earth's surface

Election Day a day set aside for people to vote for their leaders

embargo a government restriction on trade or shipping ports

employ put to work; hire

encircle to surround (in a circle)

England a European country from which many of the first settlers in America came

enslave to force people to be slaves

entwined wrapped around; laced or twisted together

evidence something used to prove something

fable a short story that teaches a lesson

Federal Triangle a large complex of public buildings that joins the Capitol to the White House

fib a childish lie

flimsy thin, easily damaged; not solid and strong

flourish a grand, sweeping movement

fossil a print or trace of a plant or animal that lived long ago, often found in layers of rock, river-beds, or other earth-crust materials

founded started, began

Fourth of July (July 4) the anniversary of the day in 1776 that America became free from England

fragile not strong; easily broken

free not under the control of another (country)

Georgetown a beautiful residential area of Washington, D.C.

gist the central thought; the main idea

graph a chart or diagram that shows the relationship between two or more things

grateful thankful, appreciative

guilty broke the law; committed a crime

gulch a deep, narrow ravine

harbor a sheltered area of a coastline where ships can dock

headquarters the offices of commanders or leaders

hoist to raise or lift into position, usually with a crane, pulley, or rope

homeland country where one was born

honor to show respect and regard

hum to sing with lips closed

hydrant a large pipe-like faucet, located at a street curb, from which water is drawn for fighting fires

indent to space in from the margin

individual one human being; a single person

industry the production of goods

infectious 1. capable of spreading disease; 2. tending to spread easily or catch on

innocent did not break the law or commit a crime

interpret to decide or explain what something means

iron a strong metal that is used in making steel

irregular not straight; uneven

jot to write down something quickly

justice fairness, rightness

kneel to rest on one or both knees

ladle a serving spoon that looks like a cup with a long handle

lag to fall behind

lawmakers people who make laws

laws rules made by a government

league a group joined together for a common purpose

"left their mark" phrase meaning that some person's or group's way of life influenced and changed something

liberty freedom

majesty the combined qualities of greatness, beauty, and dignity

majority more than half of a group

Mall (Washington) a broad walkway extending westward from the Capitol to the Potomac River beyond the Lincoln Memorial; numerous institutions are within or around the Mall, including the Smithsonian Institution, the National Gallery of Art, and the National Museum of Natural History

marsh a swampy area that is wet and soft (where tall grass and cattails often grow)

monument a structure built to honor a person or an event

motion 1. the action of moving; 2. a formal request to be decided or voted on in a meeting or trial

motto a phrase that expresses the goal or ideal

mountain ranges groups or rows of mountains

movement activity with a purpose

murmur to speak in a low voice that is hard to hear or understand

museum a building in which important objects in art, history, or science are displayed

myth a legendary or imaginary story

national belonging to a nation as a whole

neon bright colored lights used for advertising

nod to move the head up and down to signal agreement

notch a v-shaped cut, sometimes used to mark or record

ordinary average, normal

pact an agreement, contract, or treaty between people or countries

pang a quick, short pain or feeling

peach baskets bushel baskets used to store peaches

peers others of the same age or class

plight an unfortunate, difficult, or dangerous situation

Potomac River a river in east central U.S. that flows from West Virginia through Washington, D.C., into Chesapeake Bay

preacher one who speaks of religious beliefs to others

prefix letters added to the beginning of a word to change the word's meaning or use

preserve to keep or protect from harm or destruction

pride pleasure or satisfaction in one's person, accomplishments, or possessions

proof something used to show correctness or truth

proven shown to be true

pry to open with difficulty

pun a play on words (a fun way to use a word to suggest two or more of its meanings or to suggest a word that sounds similar but has a different meaning)

purity goodness; not mixed with evil

quadrants any of four equal parts

quest a hunt or search for something valuable

rebel to fight against

rebelling fighting or struggling against any kind of authority or control

rebellion action against authority

reelection the process of being voted in again

rein a narrow leather strap attached to each end of a horse's bit, used to guide and control the horse

reliable dependable (something you can count on)

religion a system of beliefs

respect honor, regard

rights privileges given a person by law or by nature

rind a hard or tough outer layer or covering (like the peeling on fruit)

river a large, natural stream (of water)

rustic plain, simple, natural; having to do with country life

salute a gesture or motion to greet or to show respect

scuff 1. to scratch up or wear a rough place on the surface; 2. to shuffle the feet when walking; to slide along

sculptor an artist who carves objects or statues out of wood, metal, stone, or clay

seal an official design used to show something is authentic

seaport a coastal town where ships can dock

seize to grab hold of; to snatch

shield an emblem or badge

shirk to avoid doing a task or job that should be done

sifting straining something to separate the larger pieces from the smaller ones; using a sieve

signer one who signs his or her name to a document

sludge soft mud or any slimy waste material

sneer a facial expression made by curling the upper lip slightly to show dislike or scorn

sniffle 1. to cry a little; 2. to have a runny nose

sobbing crying aloud with short, gasping breaths

soldier one who fights for his or her country

solve to find an explanation for or answer to

spangled sparkled or decorated with

speedy fast, quick

spur 1. a metal piece with sharp points, worn on the heel of a rider's boot, used to poke a horse to make it go; 2. anything that urges to action

steamboat a boat that runs on steam

stocker one who keeps the supplies or goods on the shelves

stow to put away or store for future use

stray 1. to wander off the path or course; 2. a lost or wandering animal

stumps 1. the stubs or short parts left after the main parts have been removed; 2. presents a problem or puzzle that someone else is unable to answer

suffixes letters added to the ends of root words to change their meanings or uses

symbols things that stand for or represent something else

talon the claw of a bird or animal

tax a payment to the government

text the printed words on a page

ton a unit of weight equal to 2000 pounds

torch a small, hand-held flaming light

tourism the practice of taking a trip to visit several points of interest for sight-seeing and pleasure

trace 1. a mark or sign left by something previously there; 2. a very small amount; 3. to copy a picture by marking its lines on a piece of thin paper placed over it; 4. to follow the clues or evidence of

traditions customs passed down from parents and grandparents

transit system a city's public transportation system, such as buses, trains, or subways

treaties formal peace or trade agreements between countries

trifle 1. something that is unimportant or has little value; 2. a small amount

trigraph three letters that come together to make one sound

U.S. Congress America's law-making group (Senate and House of Representatives)

unite to join or bring together for a common purpose

unselfish generous; not stingy

vendor one who sells

verb word or words that show action or condition

version 1. a description or report from one point of view; 2. a particular form or translation of something

Vietnam a country in SE Asia on the South China Sea which fought a communist takeover from 1955–1975

wage money paid to an employee for work done

waltz a ballroom dance for couples or the music for such a dance

weekly once every week

western boundary the edge or line down the western side

whim a sudden urge to do something for no particular reason

wick the string or cord that burns in a candle or oil lamp

Vocabulary List

(by Lesson Number)

Lesson 2

alp a high, rugged mountain

ban to prohibit or forbid

damp a little wet

lag to fall behind

Lesson 3

dim not bright; unclear

fib a childish lie

Lesson 4

jot to write down something quickly

nod to move the head up and down to signal agreement

Lesson 5

hum to sing with lips closed

pun a play on words (a fun way to use a word to suggest two or more of its meanings or to suggest a word that sounds similar but has a different meaning)

Lesson 6

text the printed words on a page

Lesson 7

clasp 1. a fastener to hold things together; 2. to hold something tightly, like to hold hands

Lesson 8

pry to open with difficulty

Lesson 9

myth a legendary or imaginary story

Lesson 10

dash 1. to run quickly; 2. a small amount

Lesson 11

chat a light, relaxed conversation

Lesson 12

con to swindle or trick

Lesson 13

wick the string or cord that burns in a candle or oil lamp

Lesson 15

indent to space in from the margin

Lesson 16	**pang** a quick, short pain or feeling
Lesson 17	**pride** pleasure or satisfaction in one's person, accomplishments, or possessions
Lesson 18	**seize** to grab hold of; to snatch
Lesson 19	**stray** 1. to wander off the path or course; 2. a lost or wandering animal
Lesson 20	**sneer** a facial expression made by curling the upper lip slightly to show dislike or scorn
Lesson 22	**verb** word or words that show action or condition
Lesson 23	**shirk** to avoid doing a task or job that should be done
Lesson 24	**murmur** to speak in a low voice that is hard to hear or understand
Lesson 25	**quest** a hunt or search for something valuable
Lesson 26	**whim** a sudden urge to do something for no particular reason
Lesson 27	**stumps** 1. the stubs or short parts left after the main parts have been removed; 2. presents a problem or puzzle that someone else is unable to answer
Lesson 28	**sifting** straining something to separate the larger pieces from the smaller ones; using a sieve
Lesson 29	**basked** took pleasure in; enjoyed a pleasant warmth
Lesson 30	**pact** an agreement, contract, or treaty between people or countries
Lesson 32	**marsh** a swampy area that is wet and soft (where tall grass and cattails often grow)
Lesson 33	**border** 1. an edge or margin; 2. the line or boundary where one thing ends and another begins
Lesson 34	**vendor** one who sells

Lesson 35 **collards** the leaves of a type of cabbage, eaten as a vegetable

Lesson 36 **fossil** a print or trace of a plant or animal that lived long ago, often found in layers of rock, riverbeds, or other earth-crust materials

Lesson 38 **dusk** late evening just before dark

Lesson 39 **proof** something used to show correctness or truth

Lesson 40 **rind** a hard or tough outer layer or covering (like the peeling on fruit)

Lesson 41 **spur** 1. a metal piece with sharp points, worn on the heel of a rider's boot, used to poke a horse to make it go; 2. anything that urges to action

Lesson 42 **stocker** one who keeps the supplies or goods on the shelves

Lesson 44 **scuff** 1. to scratch up or wear a rough place on the surface; 2. to shuffle the feet when walking; to slide along

Lesson 45 **fable** a short story that teaches a lesson

Lesson 46 **ladle** a serving spoon that looks like a cup with a long handle

Lesson 47 **trifle** 1. something that is unimportant or has little value; 2. a small amount

Lesson 48 **graph** a chart or diagram that shows the relationship between two or more things

Lesson 50 **solve** to find an explanation for or answer to

Lesson 51 **deaf** not able to hear

Lesson 52 **flimsy** thin, easily damaged; not solid and strong

Lesson 53 **kneel** to rest on one or both knees

Lesson 54 **trace** 1. a mark or sign left by something previously there; 2. a very small amount; 3. to copy a picture by marking its lines on a piece of thin paper placed over it; 4. to follow the clues or evidence of

Lesson 56 **douse** 1. to cover completely with liquid; to drench; 2. to put out (a light or fire)

Lesson 57 **stow** to put away or store for future use

Lesson 58 **hoist** to raise or lift into position, usually with a crane, pulley, or rope

Lesson 59 **embargo** a government restriction on trade or shipping ports

Lesson 60 **sobbing** crying aloud with short, gasping breaths

Lesson 62 **employ** put to work; hire

Lesson 63 **sniffle** 1. to cry a little; 2. to have a runny nose

Lesson 64 **gist** the central thought; the main idea

Lesson 65 **duty** 1. something a person must do; 2. a government tax on imported goods

Lesson 66 **weekly** once every week

Lesson 68 **plight** an unfortunate, difficult, or dangerous situation

Lesson 69 **notch** a v-shaped cut, sometimes used to mark or record

Lesson 70 **sludge** soft mud or any slimy waste material

Lesson 71 **wage** money paid to an employee for work done

Lesson 72 **gulch** a deep, narrow ravine

Lesson 74 **battle** a fight in a war

country a nation or state

dawn the beginning light of day

motion 1. the action of moving; 2. a formal request to be decided or voted on in a meeting or trial

national belonging to a nation as a whole

spangled sparkled or decorated with

Lesson 75

civil rights the equal rights of all citizens (right to liberty and freedom)

honor to show respect and regard

laws rules made by a government

preacher one who speaks of religious beliefs to others

river a large, natural stream (of water)

U.S. Congress America's law-making group (Senate and House of Representatives)

Lesson 76

citizen a resident with legal rights and protection

Election Day a day set aside for people to vote for their leaders

rights privileges given a person by law or by nature

waltz a ballroom dance for couples or the music for such a dance

Lesson 77

American colonies/colonists the first settlements in America/the first settlers

Declaration of Independence the document that declared America was free from England

England a European country from which many of the first settlers in America came

Fourth of July (July 4) the anniversary of the day in 1776 that America became free from England

rebel to fight against

unite to join or bring together for a common purpose

Lesson 78

adapt to change to make fit for a certain use

courage the quality of standing against danger or hardship; being brave

justice fairness, rightness

purity goodness; not mixed with evil

salute a gesture or motion to greet or to show respect

symbols things that stand for or represent something else

Assessment 13

homeland country where one was born

religion a system of beliefs

traditions customs passed down from parents and grandparents

Lesson 80

coding marking a word with symbols to give information about how to pronounce it

Lesson 81

auction a public sale where goods are sold to the highest bidder

capital the city where the governing bodies are located

monument a structure built to honor a person or an event

signer one who signs his or her name to a document

soldier one who fights for his or her country

Lesson 82

check a control or test

crew a team of people working together

defeated won over another, as in war

free not under the control of another (country)

interpret to decide or explain what something means

Lesson 83

appointed chosen to serve and placed in a position or office

court a group who decides issues of law

ton a unit of weight equal to 2000 pounds

Lesson 84

dome the rounded top of a building

motto a phrase that expresses the goal or ideal

rein a narrow leather strap attached to each end of a horse's bit, used to guide and control the horse

shield an emblem or badge

Assessment 14

individual one human being; a single person

lawmakers people who make laws

Lesson 86

center of trade the key place for buyers and sellers

founded started, began

grateful thankful, appreciative

movement activity with a purpose

rebellion action against authority

seaport a coastal town where ships can dock

tax a payment to the government

Lesson 87

evidence something used to prove something

guilty broke the law; committed a crime

innocent did not break the law or commit a crime

museum a building in which important objects in art, history, or science are displayed

ordinary average, normal

peers others of the same age or class

proven shown to be true

speedy fast, quick

Lesson 88

copper a soft, reddish metal that is easy to shape

harbor a sheltered area of a coastline where ships can dock

iron a strong metal that is used in making steel

liberty freedom

prefix letters added to the beginning of a word to change the word's meaning or use

sculptor an artist who carves objects or statues out of wood, metal, stone, or clay

torch a small, hand-held flaming light

Lesson 89

arena an enclosed area used for sports and other events

league a group joined together for a common purpose

suffixes letters added to the ends of root words to change their meanings or uses

peach baskets bushel baskets used to store peaches

Lesson 90

rustic plain, simple, natural; having to do with country life

Assessment 15

cornerstone a special stone laid in the foundation of a building at one of its corners when it is being built

Lesson 92

earthquake a shaking or trembling of the earth that occurs when the ground moves because of shifting rocks beneath the earth's surface

industry the production of goods

transit system a city's public transport system, such as buses, trains, or subways

version 1. a description or report from one point of view; 2. a particular form or translation of something

Lesson 93

bill a proposed law

committee a group of people assigned a certain job to do

disinfect to cleanse so as to kill disease germs

majority more than half of a group

Lesson 94

ambitious working hard to be successful

infectious 1. capable of spreading disease; 2. tending to spread easily or catch on

irregular not straight; uneven

reliable dependable (something you can count on)

steamboat a boat that runs on steam

western boundary the edge or line down the western side

Lesson 95

abolished did away with completely

baton a stick or rod used by a leader to direct

encircle to surround (in a circle)

enslave to force people to be slaves

flourish a grand, sweeping movement

unselfish generous; not stingy

Lesson 96

rebelling fighting or struggling against any kind of authority or control

Assessment 16

Broadway a famous street in New York known for its theaters

"left their mark" phrase meaning that some person's or group's way of life influenced and changed something

neon bright colored lights used for advertising

Lesson 97

district one section of an area that has been divided up for a certain purpose

hydrant a large pipe-like faucet, located at a street curb, from which water is drawn for fighting fires

reelection the process of being voted in again

respect honor, regard

Lesson 98

compiled brought together into one

entwined wrapped around; laced or twisted together

fragile not strong; easily broken

seal an official design used to show something is authentic

talon the claw of a bird or animal

treaties formal peace or trade agreements between countries

Lesson 99

archives collections of historical records and documents

Federal Triangle a large complex of public buildings that joins the Capitol to the White House

Georgetown a beautiful residential area of Washington, D.C.

headquarters the offices of commanders or leaders

Mall (Washington) a broad walkway extending westward from the Capitol to the Potomac River beyond the Lincoln Memorial; numerous institutions are within or around the Mall, including the Smithsonian Institution, the National Gallery of Art, and the National Museum of Natural History

Potomac River a river in east central U.S. that flows from West Virginia through Washington, D.C., into Chesapeake Bay

quadrants any of four equal parts

trigraph three letters that come together to make one sound

Vietnam a country in SE Asia on the South China Sea which fought a communist takeover from 1955–1975

Lesson 100

bountiful plentiful; more than is needed

Assessment 17

Continental Divide the north-to-south mountain ranges of the Rockies that divide the U.S. into east and west river flows

majesty the combined qualities of greatness, beauty, and dignity

mountain ranges groups or rows of mountains

preserve to keep or protect from harm or destruction

tourism the practice of taking a trip to visit several points of interest for sightseeing and pleasure

Sight Word List

(Alphabetized)

above
again
against
answer
any
are
aunt
beautiful
because
been
bought
brother
brought
build
busy
buy
caught
certain
climb
clothes
come
cough
could
country
course
cousin
daughter
didn't
do
does
done
don't
door
Dr.
enough
early
earth
eye
father
February
floor
fought
four
friend
from
full
give
gone
guard
guess
guest
half
have
heard
heart
hour
island
laugh
learn
listen
live
many
mother
mountain
move
Mr.
Mrs.
Ms.
none
nothing
ocean
of
often
once
one
only
other
poor
pour
prove
pull
push
put
rough
said
says
shoe
should
shoulder
sign
special
some
stomach
straight
sugar
sure
talk
tastes
taught
their
there
they
though
thought
through
to
touch
tough
trouble
two
very
walk
want
was
Wednesday
were
what
where
who
whose
woman
women
would
young

Sight Word List

(by Lesson Number)

Lesson 14

- are /ar/
- from /frŭm/
- of /ŭv/
- said /sĕd/
- to /tōō/
- want /wŏnt/
- was /wŭz/
- were /wer/
- what /hwŭt/
- where /hwĕr/

Lesson 21

- come /kŭm/
- didn't /dĭd′ nt/
- do /dōō/
- does /dŭz/
- don't /dōnt/
- one /wŭn/
- put /pŏŏt/
- says /sĕz/
- some /sŭm/
- who /hōō/

Lesson 31

- because /bĭ kŭz′/
- been /bĭn/
- could /kŏŏd/
- four /for/
- other /ŭth′ er/
- should /shŏŏd/
- their /thĕr/
- there /thĕr/
- they /thā/
- would /wŏŏd/

Lesson 37

- any /ĕn′ ē/
- brother /brŭth′ er/
- buy /bī/
- father /fŏth′ er/
- learn /lern/
- many /mĕn′ ē/
- mother /mŭth′ er/
- ocean /ō′ shŭn/
- sure /shŏŏr/
- trouble /trŭb′ əl/

Lesson 43

- again /ə gĕn′/
  - (against) /ə gĕnst′/
- door /dor/
- enough /ĭ nŭf′/
- friend /frĕnd/
- give /gĭv/
  - (live) /lĭv/
- have /hăv/
- only /ōn′ lē/
- talk /tŏk/
- walk /wŏk/
- young /yŭng/

Lesson 49

- country /kŭn′ trē/
- early /er′ lē/
- earth /erth/
- eye /ī/
- fought /fŏt/
- heard /herd/
- two /tōō/
- whose /hōōz/
- woman /wŏŏm′ ən/
- women /wĭm′ ĭn/

Lesson 55

- cousin /kŭz′ ən/
- gone /gŏn/
- guard /gard/
- guess /gĕs/
  - (guest) /gĕst/
- half /hăf/
- island /ī′ lənd/
- laugh /lăf/
- listen /lĭs′ ən/
- mountain /mŏwn′ tən/
- once /wŭns/

Lesson 61

- bought /bŏt/
- brought /brŏt/
- busy /bĭz′ ē/
- cough /kŏf/
- done /dŭn/
- rough /rŭf/
- though /thō/
- thought /thŏt/
- through /thrōō/
- tough /tŭf/

Lesson 67

- certain /ser′ tən/
- climb /klīm/
- floor /flor/
- move /mōōv/
- often /ŏ′ fən/
- push /pŏŏsh/
- shoe /shōō/
- sign /sīn/
- tastes /tāsts/
- very /vĕr′ ē/

Lesson 73

- above /ə bŭv′/
- answer /ăn′ ser/
- build /bĭld/
- caught /kŏt/
  - (taught) /tŏt/
- clothes /klōz/
- February /fĕb′ rōō-ĕr ē/
- heart /hart/
- none /nŭn/
- nothing /nŭth′ ĭng/
- straight /strāt/

Lesson 79

- beautiful /byōō′ tə-fəl/
- Dr. /dŏk′ ter/
- full /fŏŏl/
- Mrs. /mĭs′ ĭz/
- poor /pŏŏr/
- prove /prōōv/
- shoulder /shōl′ der/
- special /spĕsh′ əl/
- stomach /stŭm′ ək/
- sugar /shŏŏg′ ĕr/

Lesson 85

- aunt /ănt/
- course /kors/
- daughter /dŏ′ ter/
- hour /owr/
- Mr. /mĭs′ ter/
- Ms. /mĭz/
- pour /por/
- pull /pŏŏl/
- touch /tŭch/
- Wednesday /wĕnz′ dā/

Irregular Spelling Word List

(Alphabetized)

aboard
abstain
absurd
acclaim
accomplice
ache
achieve
acquaint
actor
adjective
admission
affirm
afloat
afraid
agile
ahead
aid
ail
aim
air
airplane
align
all
alley
almost
alphabet
already
also
altar
alter
alternate
always
ambitious
among
anchor
angular
antique
apostle
appraise
apprentice
approach
architect
archive
armor
asphalt
assign
atrocious
attaché
attack
attain
attorney
auburn
auction
audience
August
Austin
author
auto
automatic
automobile
autumn
await
awe
awful
awkward
awl
awning
bail
bait
bald
ball
balsa
barley
baseball
basketball
bayou
beach
bead
beak
beam
bean
bear
beard
beast
beat
because
beggar
beige
belief
believe
benign
bicycle
birch
bird
birdhouse
birdie
birthday
bisque
blackboard
bleach
bleak
blew
blight
blind
blizzard
bloat
bluebird
blur
blurt
board
boast
boat
bold
bolt
both
braid
Braille
brain
brawl
bread
break
breakfast
breath
breathe
brief
bright
bristle
broach
brochure
bronchitis
brontosaurus
brown
brownie
brownstone
browse
bruise
burden
burger
burglar
burlap
burly
burn
burnish
burp
burr
burro
burrow
bursar
burst
bus
bustle
buzzard
caldron
calendar
call
calm
calorie
campaign
candlelight
candor
capricious
cardboard
cashew
cashier
castle
cauliflower
cause
caution
cautious
cedar
cedilla
ceiling

WORD LISTS

celebrate
celery
cell
cellar
cement
censor
cent
center
centipede
central
century
cereal
ceremony
certain
chain
chair
chaise
chalet
chalk
chambray
chance
chandelier
chaos
chaparral
chaperone
chaps
character
charade
charcoal
Charlotte
chasm
chauffeur
cheap
cheat
chef
chemical
chew
Chicago
chief
chiffon
child
chimney
chirp
chivalry
chlorine
Chopin
choral
chord
chorus
chow mein
chowder
Chris
chrome
chronic
church
churn
chute
cider
cinch
circle
circuit
circular
circus
citizen
city
claim
clause
claw
clean
clear
cleat
clef
clique
cloak
clown
coach
coal
coarse
coast
coaster
coat
coax
cobalt
cockroach
cocoa
cold
collar
collard
collie
cologne
colt
comfort
comfortable
commission
company
compass
complain
complete
conceit
concur
concussion
condense
confession
confirm
congested
conserve
consign
consistent
constraint
consume
contain
cookie
cougar
cough
coupon
cover
coward
crawfish
crawl
creak
cream
crease
crevice
crew
critique
croak
crochet
croup
crowd
crown
cruise
crypt
crystal
curb
curd
curfew
curl
current
curse
curt
curtail
curve
custard
cycle
cyclone
cylinder
cymbal
cynic
cypress
cyst
daily
daisy
dance
dawdle
dawn
daylight
dead
deaf
deal
dealt
dear
deceive
delicious
delight
derrick
design
despair
detail
determine
dew
die
diesel
dinosaur
diphthong
dirt
disburse
discipline
discourage
discover
discussion
disturb
docile
doctor
doctrine

doe
dollar
domain
donkey
dove
down
downstairs
dowry
drain
draw
drawings
drawn
dread
dream
drew
drown
drowsy
during
each
eagle
ear
ease
east
eat
eaves
echo
eclair
eerie
eight
eighteen
eighth
eighty
either
elephant
encompass
engine
entertain
entrance
epoch
error
ewe
exalt
examine
exclaim
excursion
experience

explain
expression
extension
factor
fail
faint
fair
faith
fall
false
falter
famine
faucet
fault
fawn
fear
feast
feat
feather
feminine
femur
fence
ferocious
fervor
few
fictitious
field
fiend
fierce
fight
figurine
find
fir
fireworks
firm
first
flair
flashlight
flaunt
flaw
flea
flew
flight
flirt
float
foal

foam
foe
fold
folk
football
force
forehead
foreign
fowl
fragile
frail
fraud
freak
freedom
freight
fright
front
frontier
frown
fruit
fur
furl
furlough
furnace
furnish
furniture
further
furtive
futile
gain
gait
gall
galley
gas
gasoline
gauze
gear
genuine
geography
ghost
gird
girl
girth
gleam
gloat
glove

gnarl
gnash
gnat
gnaw
gnome
gnu
goad
goal
goalie
goat
gold
gopher
govern
government
governor
gown
gracious
grain
grammar
granular
graph
grease
great
grew
grief
grieve
grind
gristle
groan
grotesque
group
growl
gulf
gurgle
haddock
hail
hair
hall
halt
hammock
hangar
harbor
haul
haunt
hazard
head

heal
health
heap
hear
heat
heavy
high
hijack
hoard
hoarse
hoax
hockey
hoe
hold
homework
honey
horror
host
hostile
howl
hurdle
hurl
hurry
hurt
hustle
hydraulic
hyphen
if
imagine
impair
impeach
impression
infectious
infirm
instead
interview
irk
jail
jasmine
jaundice
jaw
jeans
jeer
jelly
jellyfish
jeopardy

jerk
jerky
jersey
jest
jet
jetty
jewel
jewelry
Jewish
jib
jiffy
jig
jiggle
jilt
jingle
jinx
jitter
jockey
Joe
jolt
jostle
journey
jowl
juice
justice
kangaroo
Kansas
key
kidney
kind
kingdom
kitchen
knack
knapsack
knave
knead
knee
kneecap
kneel
knell
knelt
knew
knick-knack
knife
knight
knit

knob
knock
knot
knothole
know
knowledge
knuckle
lacquer
laid
lair
lattice
laugh
launch
laundry
leach
lead
leaf
leak
lean
leap
lease
leash
least
leather
leave
leisure
liar
lie
lien
light
load
loaf
loan
loathe
loaves
London
lunar
lurch
lurk
lymph
lynx
lyric
machine
magazine
maid
mail

main
Maine
maintain
malice
malicious
mall
malt
marine
masculine
meadow
meal
mean
meant
measure
meat
mechanic
mechanism
medicine
medley
mew
might
mild
mildew
mind
mirror
mischief
mistletoe
moan
mobile
mocha
modular
mohair
mold
molt
monarch
Monday
money
monkey
month
moonlight
mortar
most
mousse
moustache
movie
much

murky
murmur
mustard
myth
nail
nausea
near
neat
nectar
nectarine
needle
neigh
neighbor
neighborhood
neither
nephew
nestle
new
newspaper
niece
nigh
night
nil
nocturnal
notice
novice
nurse
nurture
nutritious
oak
oar
oath
oatmeal
oats
oblique
oboe
obtain
occur
office
old
onyx
opaque
orchestra
orchid
ordain
orphan

outlaw
oven
overboard
overhead
owl
oxygen
paddock
paid
pail
pain
paint
pair
palsy
pamphlet
parachute
paragraph
parlor
parsley
pastor
paunch
pause
paw
pawn
pea
peach
peak
peal
peasant
pedal
percussion
permission
pernicious
perturb
petal
pew
pewter
phantom
pharmacy
phase
pheasant
phenomenon
Philadelphia
philosophy
phone
phonics
phrase

physical
physics
physique
pie
piece
pier
pierce
pillar
pint
pistachio
pitcher
plain
plaque
plea
plead
pleasant
please
pleat
plight
plus
poach
polar
police
poll
popular
possession
post
powder
practice
prairie
praise
praline
preach
precocious
prejudice
pretentious
prevail
priest
prince
proclaim
profession
progression
prophet
protein
prowl
pulley

pumice
purchase
purge
purple
purr
purse
pursue
pursuit
quad
quail
quaint
quality
quirk
raid
railroad
rain
rainbow
raise
raisin
ransack
ravine
raw
reach
read
ready
real
rear
receipt
receive
recover
refrain
refurbish
reign
rein
reindeer
relief
relieve
remain
renew
repair
repetitious
reprieve
reproach
resign
restrain
retail

retain
retrieve
return
review
rhythm
rich
ricochet
right
rind
road
roam
roar
roast
roll
rookie
rouge
rough
route
routine
rowboat
rowdy
rustle
sac
sachet
sail
sailor
saint
salt
Saturday
sauce
saucer
saw
scald
schedule
scheme
scholar
school
schooner
scowl
scream
scroll
sea
seal
seam
seat
seesaw

seize
sentence
service
sewer
shawl
shear
shield
shirk
shirt
shove
shovel
shriek
sidewalk
sigh
sight
sign
since
sir
sirloin
sis
skate
skein
skewer
skirmish
skirt
skull
skunk
slain
slaw
sleigh
slew
slight
slur
small
smear
smirk
snail
sneak
snorkel
soak
soap
soar
sold
son
soup
spacious

Spain
spawn
speak
spear
species
sphere
splendor
splurge
sponge
sprain
spread
spur
spurn
spurt
squabble
squad
squadron
squall
squander
squash
squat
squirm
squirrel
squirt
stain
stair
stall
standard
steady
steak
steal
steam
stew
stir
stomach
straight
strain
straw
strawberry
streak
stream
strew
sturdy
submarine
submission
subtle

suburb
succession
such
suit
sulphur
sunlight
superstitious
surf
surface
surge
surly
surname
surpass
surplus
surprise
survey
survive
suspension
suspicious
sustain
swab
swallow
swamp
swan
swap
swat
sweat
sweater
swirl
syllable
symbol
symptom
syntax
synthetic
syphon
system
tail
tailor
talc
talk
tall
tartar
tawny
tea
teach
teal

team
tear
tease
technical
technique
telephone
terrain
terror
thaw
thief
thigh
third
thirst
thirsty
thirty
this
thistle
thread
threat
threw
throat
through
tic
tie
tier
tight
tiptoe
toad
toast
toe
told
toll
ton
tonight
tough
toupee
tourist
towel
town
trachea
tractor
trail
train
trait
traitor
transmission
treat
trek
trestle
trolley
trough
turbine
turf
turkey
turmoil
turn
turnip
turtle
tweak
twirl
typhoid
typhoon
uncouth
uncover
unique
untie
upstairs
urban
urchin
urgency
urn
us
vain
valley
vault
veal
veil
vein
vendor
versatile
vicious
view
virtue
volatile
volley
volt
voracious
wad
waddle
waffles
wail
waist
wait
waitress
walk
wall
wallet
walnut
walrus
waltz
wand
want
wash
wasp
watch
watchful
water
watt
weak
wealth
wean
wear
weather
weave
weigh
weight
weird
which
whirl
whistle
whoa
wild
wind
withdrew
woe
won
wonder
wonderful
word
work
world
worm
worth
wound
wrack
wrangler
wrap
wrath
wreath
wreck
wren
wrench
wrestle
wretch
wriggle
wring
wrinkle
wrist
write
writhe
wrong
wrote
wrought
wrung
wry
xylophone
yawn
yea
year
yeast
yes
yield
yogurt
you
yourself
youth
zeal
zinc
zombie

Irregular Spelling Word List

(by Lesson Number)

Special Spelling Lists

/ā/

“āi” spelling

(Lesson 18)

abstain
acclaim
acquaint
afraid
aid
ail
aim
air
airplane
appraise
attain
await
bail
bait
braid
Braille
brain
campaign
chain
chair
chaise
claim
complain
constraint
contain
curtail
daily
daisy
despair
detail
domain
downstairs
drain
eclair
entertain
exclaim
explain
fail
faint
fair
faith
flair
frail
gain
gait
grain
hail
hair
impair
jail
laid
lair
maid
mail
main
Maine
maintain
mohair
nail
obtain
ordain
paid
pail
pain
paint
pair
plain
praise
prevail
proclaim
quail
quaint
raid
railroad
rain
rainbow
raise
raisin
refrain
remain
repair
restrain
retail
retain
sail
sailor
saint
slain
snail
Spain
sprain
stain
stair
straight
strain
sustain
tail
tailor
terrain
trail
train
trait
traitor
upstairs
vain
wail
waist
wait
waitress

“eā” spelling

(Lesson 51)

break
great
steak
yea

“ei” spelling

(Lesson 84)

beige
chow mein
reign
rein
reindeer
skein
veil
vein

“eigh” spelling

(Lesson 99)

eight
eighteen
eighth
eighty
freight
neigh
neighbor
neighborhood
sleigh
weigh
weight

/ē/

“ēa” spelling

(Lesson 18)

beach
bead
beak
beam
bean
beard
beast
beat
bleach
bleak
breathe
cheap
cheat
clean
clear
cleat
creak
cream
crease
deal
dear
dream
each
ear
ease

east
eat
eaves
fear
feast
feat
flea
freak
gear
gleam
grease
heal
heap
hear
heat
impeach
jeans
leach
lead
leaf
leak
lean
leap
lease
leash
least
leave
meal
mean
meat
near
neat
pea
peach
peak
peal
plea
plead
please
pleat
preach
reach
read
real
rear
scream
sea
seal
seam
seat
shear
smear
sneak
speak
spear
steal
steam
streak
stream
tea
teach
teal
team
tear
tease
treat
tweak
veal
weak
wean
weave
year
yeast
zeal

“ēi” spelling

(Lesson 18)

ceiling
conceit
deceive
either
leisure
neither
protein
receipt
receive
seize
weird

“ēy” spelling

(Lesson 18)

alley
attorney
barley
chimney
donkey
galley
hockey
honey
jersey
jockey
journey
key
kidney
medley
money
monkey
parsley
pulley
trolley
turkey
valley
volley

“iē” spelling

(Lesson 84)

achieve
belief
believe
birdie
brief
brownie
calorie
cashier
chandelier
chief
collie
cookie
diesel
eerie
field
fiend
fierce
frontier
goalie
grief
grieve
lien
movie
niece
piece
pier
pierce
prairie
priest
relief
relieve
reprieve
retrieve
rookie
shield
shriek
species
thief
tier
yield
zombie

/ĕ/

“ĕa” spelling

(Lesson 51)

ahead
already
bear
bread
breakfast
breath
dead
deaf
dealt
dread
feather
forehead
head
health
heavy

instead
lead
leather
meadow
meant
measure
overhead
peasant
pheasant
pleasant
ready
spread
steady
sweat
sweater
tear
thread
threat
wealth
wear
weather

/ī/

"ie" spelling

(Lesson 18)

die
lie
pie
tie
untie

"igh" spelling

(Lesson 68)

blight
bright
candlelight
daylight
delight
fight
flashlight
flight
fright
high
knight
light
might
moonlight
nigh
night
plight
right
sigh
sight
slight
sunlight
thigh
tight
tonight

/ĭ/

"y̆" spelling

(Lesson 8)

bicycle
crypt
crystal
cylinder
cymbal
cynic
cyst
lymph
lynx
lyric
myth
onyx
oxygen
physical
physics
rhythm
syllable
symbol
symptom
syntax
synthetic
system

/ō/

"ōa" spelling

(Lesson 18)

aboard
afloat
approach
blackboard
bloat
board
boast
boat
broach
cardboard
charcoal
cloak
coach
coal
coarse
coast
coaster
coat
coax
cockroach
cocoa
croak
float
foal
foam
gloat
goad
goal
goat
groan
hoard
hoarse
hoax
load
loaf
loan
loathe
loaves
moan
oak
oar
oath
oatmeal
oats
overboard
poach
railroad
reproach
road
roam
roar
roast
rowboat
soak
soap
soar
throat
toad
toast
whoa

"ōe" spelling

(Lesson 18)

doe
foe
hoe
Joe
mistletoe
oboe
tiptoe
toe
woe

/ŏ/

"*a* after *qu*" spelling

(Lesson 76)

quad
quality
squabble
squad
squadron

squall
squander
squash
squat

"*a* after *w*" spelling
(Lesson 76)

swab
swallow
swamp
swan
swap
swat
wad
waddle
waffles
walk
wall
wallet
walnut
walrus
wand
want
wash
wasp
watch
watchful
water
watt

"*a* before *l*" spelling
(Lesson 76)

all
almost
also
altar
alter
alternate
always
asphalt
bald
ball
balsa
baseball
basketball
caldron
call
calm
chalk
cobalt
exalt
fall
false
falter
football
gall
hall
halt
mall
malt
palsy
quality
salt
scald
sidewalk
small
squall
stall
swallow
talk
tall
walk
wall
wallet
walrus
waltz

"au" spelling
(Lesson 81)

auction
audience
August
Austin
author
auto
automatic
autumn
because
brontosaurus
cauliflower
cause
caution
clause
dinosaur
faucet
fault
flaunt
fraud
gauze
haul
haunt
hydraulic
launch
laundry
nausea
paunch
pause
sauce
saucer
vault

"aw" spelling
(Lesson 81)

awe
awful
awkward
awl
awning
brawl
claw
crawfish
crawl
dawdle
dawn
draw
drawings
drawn
fawn
flaw
gnaw
jaw
outlaw
paw
pawn
raw
saw
seesaw
shawl
slaw
spawn
straw
strawberry
tawny
thaw
yawn

/ū/

"ew" spelling
(Lesson 82)

blew
cashew
chew
crew
curfew
dew
drew
ewe
few
flew
grew
interview
jewel
knew
mew
mildew
nephew
new
newspaper
pew
pewter
renew
review

sewer
skewer
slew
stew
strew
threw
view
withdrew

"øū" spelling

(Lesson 56)

bayou
coupon
croup
discourage
group
mousse
rouge
route
routine
soup
through
toupee
tourist
uncouth
wound
you
yourself
youth

"ūɨ" spelling

(Lesson 18)

bruise
cruise
fruit
juice
pursuit
suit

/ŭ/

"Scribal *o*" spelling

(Lesson 83)

among
comfort
comfortable
company
compass
complete
condense
confirm
congested
conserve
consistent
consume
cover
discover
dove
encompass
freedom
front
frontier
glove
govern
government
governor
kingdom
London
Monday
money
monkey
month
oven
phantom
recover
shove
shovel
son
sponge
ton
uncover
won
wonder
wonderful

/er/

"ar" spelling

(Lesson 35)

altar
angular
beggar
blizzard
burglar
bursar
buzzard
calendar
cedar
cellar
circular
collar
collard
cougar
coward
custard
dollar
grammar
granular
hangar
hazard
jeopardy
liar
lunar
modular
mortar
mustard
nectar
pillar
polar
popular
standard
tartar

"ir" spelling

(Lesson 23)

affirm
birch
bird
birdhouse
birthday
bluebird
chirp
circle
circuit
circus
confirm
dirt
fir
firm
first
flirt
gird
girl
girth
infirm
irk
quirk
shirk
shirt
sir
sirloin
skirmish
skirt
smirk
squirm
squirrel
squirt
stir
swirl
third
thirst
thirsty
thirty
twirl
virtue
whirl

"or" spelling
(Lesson 34)

actor
armor
candor
doctor
error
factor
fervor
fireworks
harbor
homework
horror
mirror
parlor
pastor
splendor
terror
tractor
vendor
word
work
world
worm
worth

"ur" spelling
(Lesson 24)

absurd
auburn
blur
blurt
burden
burger
burglar
burlap
burly
burn
burnish
burp
burr
burro
burrow
bursar
burst
church
churn
concur
curb
curd
curfew
curl
current
curse
curt
curtail
curve
disburse
disturb
during
excursion
femur
fur
furl
furlough
furnace
furnish
furniture
further
furtive
gurgle
hurdle
hurl
hurry
hurt
lurch
lurk
murky
murmur
nocturnal
nurse
nurture
occur
perturb
purchase
purge
purple
purr
purse
pursue
refurbish
return
Saturday
slur
splurge
spur
spurn
spurt
sturdy
suburb
sulphur
surf
surface
surge
surly
surname
surpass
surplus
surprise
survey
survive
turbine
turf
turkey
turmoil
turn
turnip
turtle
urban
urchin
urgency
urn
yogurt

/ow/

"ow" spelling
(Lesson 57)

brown
brownie
brownstone
browse
chowder
clown
crowd
crown
down
downstairs
dowry
drown
drowsy
fowl
frown
gown
growl
howl
jowl
owl
powder
prowl
rowdy
scowl
towel
town

/ch/

Irregular *tch* and *ch* spellings
(Lesson 72)

kitchen
much
pitcher
rich
such
which

/f/

"ph" spelling
(Lesson 48)

alphabet
asphalt
diphthong
elephant
geography
gopher
graph
hyphen
nephew
orphan
pamphlet
paragraph
phantom
pharmacy
phase
pheasant
phenomenon
Philadelphia
philosophy
phone
phonics
phrase
physical
physics
prophet
sphere
sulphur
syphon
telephone
typhoid
typhoon
xylophone

/j/

Irregular /j/ spelling
(Lesson 64)

adjective
jeans
jeer
jelly
jellyfish
jerk
jerky
jersey
jest
jet
jetty
jewel
jewelry
Jewish
jib
jiffy
jig
jiggle
jilt
jingle
jinx
jitter

/k/

"Greek *ch*" spelling
(Lesson 11)

ache
anchor
architect
archive
bronchitis
chaos
character
chasm
chemical
chlorine
choral
chord
chorus
Chris
chrome
chronic
echo
mechanic
mechanism
mocha
monarch
orchestra
orchid
schedule
scheme
scholar
school
schooner
technical
trachea

Irregular initial/medial /k/ spelling
(Lesson 12)

kangaroo
Kansas
lacquer
skate
skull
skunk

Irregular final /k/ spelling
(Lessons 13, 38, 90)

antique
attack
bisque
clique
critique
derrick
epoch
grotesque
haddock
hammock
hijack
monarch
oblique
opaque
paddock
physique
plaque
ransack
sac
stomach
talc
technique
tic
trek
unique
zinc

/s/

"Cedilla *c*" spelling
(Lesson 54)

audience
cedar
cedilla
celebrate
celery
cell
cellar
cement
censor
cent
center
centipede
central
century
cereal
ceremony
certain
chance
cider
cinch

circle
circus
citizen
city
cycle
cyclone
cylinder
cymbal
cynic
cypress
cyst
dance
entrance
experience
fence
force
prince
sauce
saucer
sentence
since

/sh/

"French *ch*" spelling

(Lesson 11)

attaché
brochure
chaise
chalet
chambray
chandelier
chaparral
chaperone
chaps
charade
Charlotte
chauffeur
Chicago
chiffon
chivalry
Chopin
chute
crochet
machine
moustache
parachute
pistachio
ricochet
sachet

/shŭn/

"[sion" spelling

(Lesson 92)

admission
commission
concussion
confession
discussion
expression
extension
impression
percussion
permission
possession
profession
progression
submission
succession
suspension
transmission

/shŭs/

"[cious" spelling

(Lesson 94)

atrocious
capricious
delicious
ferocious
gracious
malicious
pernicious
precocious
spacious
suspicious
vicious
voracious

"[tious" spelling

(Lesson 94)

ambitious
cautious
fictitious
infectious
nutritious
pretentious
repetitious
superstitious

Special Spelling Lists

"Wild Colt" words

(Lesson 40)

blind
bold
bolt
both
child
cold
colt
find
fold
folk
ghost
gold
grind
hold
host
jolt
kind
mild
mind
mold
molt
most
old
pint
poll
post
rind
roll
scroll
sign
sold
told
toll
volt
wild
wind

Final, stable syllables

(Lesson 63)

apostle
bristle
bustle
castle
eagle
gristle
hustle
jostle
mistletoe
needle
nestle
pedal
petal
rustle
snorkel
subtle
thistle
trestle
whistle
wrestle

Ghost letter digraph "gn"

(Lesson 53)

align
assign
benign
campaign
cologne
consign
design
foreign
gnarl
gnash
gnat
gnaw
gnome
gnu
reign
resign
sign

Ghost letter digraph "kn"

(Lesson 53)

knack
knapsack
knave
knead
knee
kneecap
kneel
knell
knelt
knew
knick-knack
knife
knight
knit
knob
knock
knot
knothole
know
knowledge
knuckle

Ghost letter digraph "wr"

(Lesson 53)

wrack
wrangler
wrap
wrath
wreath
wreck
wren
wrench
wrestle
wretch
wriggle
wring
wrinkle
wrist
write
writhe
wrong
wrote
wrought
wrung
wry

Floss words

(Lesson 44)

bus
chef
clef
cough
gas
graph
gulf
if
laugh
mischief
nil
plus
rough
sis
this
tough
trough
us
yes

French ending "*-ice*"

(Lesson 98)

accomplice
apprentice
crevice
jaundice
justice
lattice
malice
notice
novice
office
police
practice
prejudice
pumice
service

French ending "*-ile*"

(Lesson 98)

agile
automobile
docile
fragile
futile
hostile
mobile
versatile
volatile

French ending "*-ine*"

(Lesson 98)

chlorine
determine
discipline
doctrine
engine
examine
famine
feminine
figurine
gasoline
genuine
imagine
jasmine
machine
magazine
marine
masculine
medicine
nectarine
praline
ravine
routine
submarine

Prefixes

Prefix	Definition	Example(s)
a-	on; in; at	ablaze
ab-	from; away; off	abnormal
ad-	to; toward	adjust
al-	to; toward	almost
amphi-	around; both	amphitheater
an-	without; not	anarchy
ana-	backward; against	anagram
ante-	before	antedate
anti-	against	antiglare
astro-	star	astronaut
auto-	done by oneself	autograph
be-	by; quite; much; exist	below
bi-	two	bicycle, biceps
bio-	life	biosphere
com-	with; together	compile
con-	with; together	conform
contra-	against	contradiction
de-	down; from; undo	depart
dia-	through	diameter
dis-	not; opposite	disbelieve, disjoin
en-	to make	encircle
ex-	from; out of	export
for-	involving failure or neglect	forget
fore-	prior to	foresee
geo-	earth	geosciences
hemi-	half	hemisphere
hyper-	over; more than normal	hypertension
im-	in, not, or without	impossible
in-	in, not, or without	inborn, insecure
inter-	between; among	intertwine

intra-	inside; within	intrastate
ir-	in, not, or without	irregular
micro-	small	microscope
mini-	very small; little	minibus
mis-	wrong	misplace
mono-	one	monocle, monologue
multi-	many	multilevel
non-	not	nonfat
ob-	against; to; toward	obverse
out-	beyond; exceeds	outdoors
over-	beyond; too much	overpay, overuse
para-	by the side of; around	parachute
pent-	five	pentagon, pentagram
per-	through; completely	peruse
peri-	around	periscope
photo-	produced by light	photograph
poly-	many	polygraph
post-	after	postgame
pre-	before	precook, prefix
pro-	for; forward; in the direction of	proclaim
quad-	four	quadrigraph, quadruplets
re-	back; again	retest
retro-	before; back	retroactive
self-	by a person or thing unaided	self-taught
semi-	half; partial	semisweet
sub-	under; after	subway
super-	above; more than	superstar
syn-	together	synthesis
trans-	across	transport
tri-	three	triangle, trigraph, tricycle
un-	not; opposite	undo, uneven
under-	below; not enough	underestimate, underpay

Suffixes

Suffix	Definition	Example(s)
-able	is	dependable
-age	act; state of	bandage, drainage
-al	like; act of	musical
-an	one who	American
-ance	state of; act of	brilliance
-ancy	state of; act of	truancy
-ant	one who; that which	attendant
-ar	one who; like	liar
-ary	place where	secondary
-ate	to make	associate
-dom	state of; condition of	freedom
-ed	already happened	filled, jumped
-ee	one who; one to whom	absentee
-en	made of …; to cause to have or become	wooden, deepen
-ence	state of; act of	reference
-ency	state of; act of	agency
-er	more than; one who …	shorter, baker
-ery	a place to; practice or condition	winery
-es	more than one; plural	bushes, boxes
-est	the most; superlative	slowest, fullest
-ful	full of; quantity that will fill …	peaceful, capful
-fy	to make	beautify
-hood	state of	boyhood
-ible	able or capable	responsible
-ic	relating to; like	poetic
-ing	happening now	filling, jumping
-ish	nationality; somewhat like …	British, childish
-ism	action, process, or practice	heroism
-ist	one who …	feminist, cartoonist
-ity	state of; act of	senility

-ive	inclined to	attractive
-ize	to make	specialize
-less	without	hatless, jobless
-let	small one; article worn on	starlet, wristlet
-ly	like; how; occurring at a specified time	sadly, quickly, daily
-ment	having the quality of	merriment
-ment	state of; act of	judgment
-ness	state of; condition of	redness, sadness
-or	one who; that which	dictator
-ory	place where	observatory
-ous	having; full of	odorous, humorous
-s	more than one; plural	pants, sacks
-some	inclined to	lonesome
-ty	state of; act of	frailty
-y	like; state of; place that; small	healthy, angry, saddlery, puppy

Glossary of Phonics Terms

accent the syllable receiving the primary stress in a word

blend (verb) to combine the letter sounds in a word in order to pronounce it; (noun) two consonants that slide together very smoothly (the *pl* in *play*; the *sk* in *skip*)

bossy *r* a letter *r* that follows a vowel and changes the sound that vowel would normally make (the *r* in *arm*)

bossy *w* a letter *w* that appears by certain letters and changes the sound those letters would normally make (the *w* in *worm* or *warm*)

breve a coding mark used to indicate a vowel's short sound; looks like a "smile" (ă)

cedilla a coding mark on the letter *c* used to indicate its soft sound, as in *cent* (ç)

changing rule a spelling rule stating that when a word ends with a consonant and a *y*, change *y* to *i* before adding a suffix, except for suffixes beginning with *i* (*silly* plus *-ness*: *silliness*)

code to mark a word with symbols to give information about how to pronounce it

combination two letters that come together to make an unexpected sound (the *qu* in *quick*; the *ir* in *shirt*)

consonant digraph two consonants representing one consonant sound (the *th* in *bath*; the *sh* in *shark*); a digraph

consonant suffix a suffix that begins with a consonant (*-less*; *-ful*)

controlled vocabulary decodable text containing only those letters, letter clusters, and sounds that have been taught (See also *decodable text*)

decodable text text that can be deciphered following phonetic rules

decode to interpret the phonetic code in order to read it

derivative a root word with something added to it, such as a suffix or prefix

digraph two letters that come together to make one sound (the *ck* in *lock*; the *aw* in *straw*)

diphthong two vowel sounds that come together so fast that they are considered one syllable (the *oi* in *coin*)

doubling rule a spelling rule stating that when the final syllable of a root word is accented, and it ends with one vowel and one consonant, double the final consonant before adding a vowel suffix (*hit* plus *-ing*: *hitting*)

dropping rule a spelling rule stating that when a root word ends with a silent *e*, drop the *e* before adding a vowel suffix (*make* plus *-ing*: *making*)

explicit, systematic phonics a method of phonics instruction in which sound-spelling correspondences are taught directly and then practiced using decodable text; often includes a phonemic awareness component and emphasizes the importance of prompt feedback from the teacher (See also *decodable text*; *phonemic awareness*; *phonics*; *sound-spelling correspondence*)

final the last sound, letter(s), or position in a word

final, stable syllable a nonphonetic syllable that occurs in the final position frequently enough to be considered stable (the *ble* in *crumble*; the *tion* in *lotion*)

floss rule a spelling rule stating that the letters *f, l,* and *s* are doubled after a short vowel in a one-syllable root word (*puff*; *hiss*; *ball*)

ghost letters letters whose sounds are no longer pronounced in certain letter combinations (the *gn* in *gnat*; the *kn* in *knife*; the *wr* in *write*)

initial the first sound, letter(s), or position in a word

k-back a vertical line on the back of a *c* representing the /k/ sound, as in *cat* (c)

long vowel the vowel sounds heard in the following: *a* in *cake*; *e* in *me*; *i* in *ivy*; *o* in *open*; and *u* in *unicorn*; the sound is the same as the vowel's name

macron a coding mark used to indicate a vowel's long sound; looks like an overline (ā)

medial the middle sound(s), letter(s), or position in a word

phoneme the smallest meaningful sound unit in a word (the word *risk* contains four phonemes—/r/-/ĭ/-/s/-/k/; *play* contains only three—/p/-/l/-/ā/)

phonemic awareness an awareness that words are composed of separate sounds and the ability to hear and manipulate those sounds; an essential pre-reading skill

phonics a method of teaching beginners how to read by learning the sounds each letter and letter cluster makes and the rules governing the use of those sounds (See also *explicit, systematic phonics*)

possessive *s* an apostrophe *s* added to a word to show ownership (*Pat's frog*)

prefix a letter or group of letters added to the beginning of a root word that changes the meaning or usage of the word

quadrigraph four letters that come together to make one sound (the *eigh* in *sleigh*)

regular for reading a term used to describe a sound that a letter or group of letters makes at least 85% of the time

regular for spelling a term used to describe a spelling that occurs at least 85% of the time

root word a word with no prefix or suffix added; also referred to as a *base word*

schwa a coding mark placed over a vowel to indicate the short *u* sound (å)

short vowel the vowel sounds heard in the following: *a* in *cat*; *e* in *bed*; *i* in *zip*; *o* in *pot*; and *u* in *sun*

sight word a word in which all or part does not follow phonetic rules

silent *e* the *e* that makes the vowel say its long sound (the *e* in *snake*); also any *e* that makes no sound; usually found in the final position of an English root word

sound-spelling correspondence the relationship between the sound a letter or letter cluster makes and how the sound is spelled

suffix a letter or group of letters added to the end of a root word that changes the meaning or usage of the word

syllable a word or part of a word that contains only one vowel sound and is made by one impulse of the voice

syllable division the breaking of a word into separate syllables to make decoding (pronunciation) easier

trigraph three letters that come together to make one sound (the *igh* in *sigh*; the *dge* in *bridge*)

twin consonants two adjacent consonants that are just alike (the *tt* in *butter*)

voice line a horizontal line through the middle of a letter representing a voiced sound (s)

voiced sound a sound that requires use of the vocal cords; a vibration is felt

vowel digraph two vowels representing one vowel sound (the *ai* in *rain*; the *oa* in *soap*); a digraph

vowel rules rules that determine a vowel's sound in a given situation in a syllable

vowel suffix a suffix that begins with a vowel (*-ing*; *-ed*)

"Wild Colt" words words containing the letters *i* or *o* followed by two consonants; the vowels are often pronounced with their long sounds (*wild*; *mold*)